# GRACE MERCY and LOVE

WRITTEN BY

# MAXINE CHISHOLM

Printed in the United States of America

ISBN:    Hardcover          978-1-63871-519-1
         Softcover          978-1-63871-517-7
         eBook              978-1-63871-518-4

Republished by: PageTurner Press and Media LLC
Publication Date: 09/02/2021

**To order copies of this book, contact:**

PageTurner Press and Media
Phone: 1-888-447-9651
info@pageturner.us
www.pageturner.us

# *Acknowledgment:*

First and always, I give all the Glory, Honor, and Praises to God, the All-Powerful One, the GREAT I AM who breathed life in me and is the head of my life. Thank you, Heavenly Father, for giving me the gift to be able to write this book, and for allowing the Holy Spirit to force me to write this book. Although writing was just a hobby of mine, I never had any intention of becoming an Author.

*"For I know the plans I have for you," declares the LORD, "plans to prosper you, plans to give you hope and a future." – Jeremiah 29:11 (NIV)*

It was you, Father God, that gave me this gift of writing. While the Holy Spirit showed me everything to write in this book from the first page to the last page, I had to be obedient; allowing no one or anything to get in my way. By writing this book, I am confessing to the world that I was convicted by the Holy Spirit to expose my sins, because I would have just swept them under a rug and never went back to clean it up; but the Holy Spirit came to my house (my heart) and snatched the dirty rug (my sins) from under me and forced me to write this book (my confession). I am not afraid nor am I ashamed to tell the world that I am a sinner, saved by God's **GRACE**, and His **MERCY**.

# *"Thank You."*

Thank you, Heavenly Father God, for never leaving me nor forsaking me. After failing miserably at life, Father God, you sent me help; a friend. You didn't just send me any friend, but a very special friend that You personally hand-picked. You sent me a man of God, an amazing and a true friend of almost 23 years.

Thank you Rev. John J. Davis, Senior Pastor and Teacher of Iconium Missionary Baptist Church for being obedient and never questioning God but willingly stepped up to the plate to be a great friend to me.  Even though you witnessed a lot of what I was going through during my messy divorce; back in September 2001, you never judged me. You never looked down on me, nor left me to figure things out on my own. You didn't mind the task that God had placed on you; and, you never once got mad or angry, nor did you complain. You made me feel special, beautiful, and good about myself and you taught me how to love myself; again. Thank you so much John for allowing God to use you to help me so that I was able to move on with my life; you were the perfect gentleman. Also, thank you, so much, Rev. John J. Davis for proofreading my book for me and for being there for me when my mother passed away. You are my #1 Fan and my best friend for life.

I also want to say, 'Thank you' to everyone in advance who believed in me and help published my book; you guys helped made my story come to life. I truly appreciate everything that all of you guys did for me at PageTurner Press and Media.

Ronel Garces, Senior Author Advisor, and my Book Agent

Michael Turner – Account Executive

Christopher Samson, Production Manager

Marie Mortalla - Production Coordinator

Christian Edulan – Marketing Coordinator

Raymart Ybanez – Support Officer, and

Clarisse Arch – Publicity and Marketing Specialist

*Synopsis:*

While writing this non-fictional book of true Testimonies about my life, it was the hardest thing that I ever had to do; crying, while re-living and re-writing my past, and seeing my life in black and white; was self-crucifixion. The Holy Spirit made me write this book to expose myself; to use me as an example, to help someone out there, who feels like all hope is gone.

So, as I am ministering to you, I am also ministering to myself. Living my life is one thing, but writing this book made me realize how much of a sinner that I truly was; I was hard-headed, stubborn, disobedient, didn't like to be told what to do; just one sin after another. Yes, the Lord chastised me; but He didn't kill me. Although, my life was not perfect but rather pure hell, I'd ask myself, why does God love me so much?

The Holy Spirit is using my life story as a Testimony to help save someone, who is ready to give up and throw in the towel, for them to see that they too can be an overcomer. Trust me, I'd been there; molested as a child, homeless, escaped death twice, suicidal, in an abusive marriage: mentally and physically. I hated myself and I question God; why? Some days, I cried all day and all night, regretting the day that I was born.

Then there were other times, that I thought that I had messed up so bad with God, that God had ran out of Mercies for me. Going through one storm after another, one trial after another, only to have failed them over and over and over. In spite of my many failures, God didn't give up on me. He was right there pruning me, shaping me and molding me to be His masterpiece; so, He can get all of the Glory out of my life.

He used my life's experiences as an open-book, to let someone out there know that He is right there with you. While you are going through your storms; which is your Ministry, He promise to never leave you, nor forsake you; if you don't believe me, read my book for yourself. I am just a sinner saved by God's **Grace**, His **Mercy** and His unconditional **Love**. He is the Alpha and Omega- the beginning, and the end.

# *About the Author:*

**Maxine Chisholm:** Born in Florida but raised in Michigan, she is the second oldest of four daughters; whereas, her mom raised all of them by herself. She is a happily divorced mother of over 20 years with three amazing, and handsome sons, three beautiful daughters-in-law and ten awesome and wonderful grandchildren. She always wanted a big family; whereas, God had blessed her with, through her sons.

Although, she is a Children's Book Author, the Holy Spirit led her to write this non-fictional book of her true-life Testimonies. She faced many challenges at the young age of seven; upon, relocating to Michigan. While going through the fire, she knew that she was meant to bend, but not break. And, in spite of her many down falls, God still loved her and granted her unmerited favors.

You can also check out her other books, "Now, You Shut Op!," "The Bully Versus The prophet," and "A'Niyah's Book on Grandmas." Also, check out her other sites below:

*Website: www.maxinechisholmbooks.com*

*FaceBook: Maxine Chisholm*

*Twitter: @ladymax513*

*Instagram: maxinec13*

# TABLE OF CONTENTS

# *How to Pray*

*Jesus told us how we ought to pray in the Bible in Matthew 6:9-15 (KJV): 6. But thou, when thou prayest, enter into thy closet, and when thou hast shut the door, pray to the Father which is in secret; and thy Father which seeth in secret shall reward thee openly. This then, is how you should pray:*

*"Our Father which art in heaven, Hallowed be thy name.*
*Thy kingdom come. Thy will be done*
*in earth, as it is in heaven.*
*Give us this day our daily bread.*
*And forgive us our debts, as we forgive our debtors.*
*And lead us not into temptation, but deliver us from evil:*
*For thine is the kingdom,*
*And the power, and the glory*
*Forever. Amen."*

Jesus also said in verses 14 & 15; "For if ye forgive men their trespasses, your heavenly Father will also forgive you: But if ye forgive not men their trespasses, neither will your Father forgive your trespasses."

In Matthew 18:21-22 it says: *"Then came Peter to him, and said, Lord how oft shall my brother sin against me, and I forgive him? Til seven times? Jesus saith unto him, I say not unto thee, until seven times: but, until seventy times seven."*

I quoted all of that from the Bible just to say this, our Heavenly Father God already know what we have need of before we come to Him and ask of him, Jesus wants us to forgive all day long when anyone wrongs us, no matter the circumstances. It doesn't matter who said what or who started it or who instigated it; I know from experience that when someone wrongs me, the first thing I want to do is get even and repent later but wrong is wrong, and no wrong outweighs the other. God is listening and watching everything that we are doing down here on earth; be it good or bad, everything is being recorded in Heaven. God wants us to be the bigger person and live peaceably with everyone; so, swallow your pride and forgive, if you want to be forgiven; besides, you don't want to stand before God on Judgement Day and hear Him say, "Get away from me, you people who do wrong. I never knew you." Matthew 7:23 (ERV)

# *The Ten Commandments:*

*Exodus 20 (KJV) And GOD spoke all these words, saying, I am the LORD thy God, which have brought thee out of the land of Egypt, out of the house of bondage.*

1.  *Thou shalt have no other gods before me.*
2.  *Thou shalt not make unto thee any graven image or any likeness of anything that is in heaven above, or that is in the earth beneath, or that is in the water under the earth. Thou shall not bow down thyself to them, nor serve them: for I the LORD thy God am a jealous God, visiting the iniquity of the fathers upon the children unto the third and fourth generation of them that hate me. And shewing mercy unto thousands of them that love me, and keep my commandments.*
3.  *Thou shalt not take the name of the LORD thy God in vain; for the LORD will not hold him guiltless that taketh his name in vain.*
4.  *Remember the sabbath day, to keep it holy. Six days shalt thou labour, and do all thy work. But the seventh day is the sabbath of the Lord thy God: in it thou shalt not do any work, thou, nor thy son, nor thy daughter, thy manservant, nor thy maidservant, nor thy cattle, nor thy stranger that is within thy gates.  For in six days the LORD made heaven and earth, the sea, and all that in them is, and rested the seventh day: wherefore the LORD blessed the sabbath day, and hallowed it.*
5.  *Honour thy father and thy mother: that thy days may be long upon the land which the LORD thy God giveth thee.*
6.  *Thou shalt not kill.*
7.  *Thou shalt not commit adultery.*
8.  *Thou shalt not steal.*
9.  *Thou shalt not bear false witness against thy neighbour.*
10.  *Thou shalt not covet (means to possess or to have) thy neighbour's house, thou shall not covet thy neighbour's wife, nor his manservant, nor his maidservant, nor his ox, nor his ass, nor any thing that is thy neighbour's.*

# Confessing your Sins and the Prayer of Faith

*James 5:15-16 (BSB) 15. "And the prayer offered in faith will restore the one who is sick. The Lord will raise him up. If he has sinned, he will be forgiven. 16. Therefore confess your sins to each other and pray for each other so that you may be healed. The prayer of a righteous man has great power to prevail."*

As I was led by the Holy Spirit to write this book, I am truly thankful and grateful to God for showing me Mercy. He could have taken my life a long time ago, but instead, granted me unmerited favors. I realize that His love for me is far greater than I can ever imagine. Living my life is one thing, but seeing my life in black and white made me realize how much of a sinner I truly was; I was hard-headed, stubborn and didn't like to be told what to do; But God didn't let go of me. Yes, I messed up, I did wrong, but He didn't kill me; He could have, if He wanted to. It was His unconditional love for me is what kept me. God love us so much that He allowed His only begotten son, Jesus, to lay down His life for us. He said it best about us in Isaiah 64:6.

*Isaiah 64:6 (KJV); "But we are all like an unclean thing, and all our righteousnesses are like filthy rags; and we do fade as a leaf; and our iniquities, like the wind, have taken us away."*

Regardless of how much we mess up, God is full of Mercies and His Mercies endure forever. In spite, of the filthy rags that God says we are, He still loves us. He wants nothing but the best for his children. I messed up so bad with God that I thought God had ran out of Mercies for me. I hated myself; I sometimes cried all day and all night regretting the day that I was born, I cursed the day that I entered into this mean and nasty world; because I had messed up with God so bad, one sin after another just continuing to be disobedient.

I truly believe that the Holy Spirit wanted me to write this book to expose my life; to use me as an example, as an open book, to help someone out there who feels like all hope is gone. Because I never wanted to expose myself or my life style, I truly believe the Holy Spirit wanted to use me to help save someone who is ready to give up and throw in the towel. Don't be angry with God, but trust in Him, even when you can't see the light at the end of the tunnel.

Everything written in this book is true; it's non-fictional, and God is using my life story as a testimony to help someone see that they too can be an overcomer.  So, put on your spiritual seat belt and hold on tight because some of the things that I am about to share and confess with you are mind-blowing, but by confessing our sins one to another, we are being healed, and set free. God forgives, because He's the same God, yesterday, today and forever more.  He's still in the healing business and He still cares and love us no matter how much we think we'd messed up with him.

*"For my thoughts are not your thoughts, neither are your ways my ways," saith the LORD. For as the heavens are higher than the earth, so are my ways higher than your ways, and my thoughts than your thoughts." Isaiah 55:8-9 (KJV)*

# "RECEIVING THE HOLY GHOST."

*Acts 2:38 And Peter said to them, "Repent and be baptized every one of you in the name of Jesus Christ for the forgiveness of your sins, and you will receive the gift of the Holy Spirit."*

Looking back when I was 25 years young, having three sons; the first two out of wedlock, not married and as my father-in-law would say, "living in sin, fornicating." I got married to the man of all three of my sons, six months after we had our second son and because number one, I wanted to make things right with God. Number two, so people could stop looking down on me; having my co-workers to have to sneak and give me a baby shower after giving birth to my first son; back in the 80's, they couldn't congratulate me on my new born baby because I had him out of wedlock; I was looked down upon like a filthy rag that God says that we are. I was truly hurt, especially, since my baby's daddy mother had to sneak and come see my sons. My boyfriend's dad, wouldn't allow me to bring my babies over to his house because his son and I were living in sin; not married, "shacking up" as the old folks would say. He would say hurtful things to me when he found out that I was pregnant, "I guess you proud of yourself, you brought your little fast tail over here and raped my son. Don't bring that bastard over here, y'all over there living in sin."

His words ripped me apart on the inside, but once his son and I got married, my in-laws were my best friends; they loved my sons and babysat for us while we worked and to help us out so we can save our money. My father-in-law did apologize to me for all the hurtful things he said. He would tease with me and say, "Max, you're my favorite daughter-in-law," as he started cracking up laughing. And, I would say back to him, "That's because, I'm your only daughter-in-law." None of his sons were married; except for my husband. He told me that I was the best thing that ever happened to his son because he noticed that once I started coming around, that his son was staying out of trouble.

He told me that he was angry because we were living together, not married and having babies. He just wanted us to get married and he gave me $1,000 in cash that he was saving up to give to us once we got married but seeing that I didn't have a ring, he told me to go and buy myself a nice ring; back in 1985, that was a lot of money. I only got to buy myself a ring for $99 dollars because, my husband took the money, gave me a $100 and said that I didn't need no expensive ring and we had bills to pay; the truth be told, we didn't have a lot of debts, we paid for everything with cash and paid our bills on time; sometime, we over paid on our accounts, having credit on our accounts. We had no credit which was why it was hard for us to get anything but we didn't care, we just didn't want to owe anyone anything.

My in-laws watched all of our sons and all of their other grandchildren as well; we never had to pay for daycare, and they weren't about to let anyone one else watch them. My mother-in-law no longer had to sneak to come to see my sons; shortly thereafter, I left my former church and joined my husband's church, I got baptized and I received the washing of my feet. But I never received the Holy Ghost nor spoke in tongues. I was so disappointed and hurt after having done all of those things, and not one person at the church called me, or offered encouragement to assist me in my walk with Christ. In order to be baptized, I had to be a faithful (tithing) member, so I did all of the requirements because I was serious about accepting Christ in my heart, my home and my life.

After months went by and my husband had gone to work, I was anxious about putting the kids to bed early. I wanted to have me some me time, to pray and talk to God about the way I was feeling; besides, I had no one to talk to, I didn't trust people enough to talk to them. I didn't want no one to know my business because they would have spread it all over the church. So, I hurried up and went into the living room and got down on my knees, with my hands together and before I could say one word, the Holy Ghost fell on me; I couldn't move, I couldn't even speak. I just laid on the sofa and allowed the Holy Ghost to take over. When I tell you that the Holy Ghost took over, it was an indescribable feeling. I mean, it was such an awesome feeling that I had never experienced before; no man on this earth could have made me feel the way the Holy Ghost made me feel. I didn't want that feeling to never go away, I went to bed thinking about that Holy Ghost encounter.

The next day, I hurried and put the kids to bed and ran in the living room and got down on my knees again and again and again for days just so that the Holy Ghost can take over my body. The feeling was so indescribable that there were no words to explain the feeling, you just have to get saved and baptize and try the Holy Ghost for yourself; you won't be disappointed, but wished that you had received the Holy Ghost a long time ago. All I could do at other times were raised my hands and praise God, I truly forgot what I wanted to talk to God about because praising Him was all that I wanted to do.

After my encounter was over for that night, I went to bed thinking that I was in heaven. If you have never met the Holy Spirit, ask for Him. The all-time great and anointed Gospel singer and Pastor, Shirley Caesar said it best in her song, "I Remember Momma," oh how I love all of her songs but "I Remember Momma," is my favorite one.

When she said in her song, "I don't care who you are, you can be the chief of sinners, but you will never be the same once you come in contact with God."

# "GOD GRANTED ME GRACE AND MERCY."

*Grace is a gift we don't deserve.*
*Mercy is not getting the punishment we deserve.*
*Ephesians 2:4-10 (KJV)*

God granted me Grace and Mercy; even though, I didn't deserve it. He gave me a second chance. You will read about that in, "Testimony #11." One night, I was 25 years old at the time, I went to bed and all of a sudden, a man came into my bedroom and turned on the light. This man was dressed in an all pure white and super bright robe said to me, "Come, you must go now, it's your time to go."

"What do you mean it's my time to go?" I asked.

"You must go now," he said.

"Wait! I'll go, but first let me get my children," I said, whom at that time were one, three and five years of age.

"No, you must come alone," he said.

While trying to see his face, I couldn't because the light was so bright, I immediately sat up and turned to my husband and said, "Honey, wake up! There's a man in our bedroom, tell him to turn off the light. It's too bright, I can't see," while shaking him trying to wake him up.

"He can't hear you," the man said.

"What do you mean he can't hear me?" I asked.

"Because you are dead," he said.

As I turned my head around, while still sitting up in my bed, I looked back and saw myself still laying down in the bed. I panic and said, "No! No! I won't go." The man immediately took his hand, turned off the light switch in my bedroom and disappeared.

Now, I don't know what death feels like, but I can assure you that it would had been better for me to go, than to come back from the dead; it was worse than giving birth. I screamed once he turned the light off, I just remember being in so much pain. I was bent over in a fetus position, screaming. My husband woke up and said, "Max, what's wrong?

"Give me something to eat, I just came back from the dead," I said.

"Max, you had a bad dream," he said.

"No, you don't understand. I died in my sleep, I am in a lot of pain; give me something to eat," I said. I was so hungry that it felt like I was about to die; again.

"Max, you had a nightmare," he said.

Fast forward, ten years later: An angel, a female voice, visited me in my sleep and said, "Ten years ago, you had an outer body experience, where you died in your sleep."

"Yes," I said.

"God granted you 25 more years onto your life, so, at the age of 50 you shall surely die," said the Angel.

In Romans 3:23 (NIV) the scripture says, "*For all have sinned and fall short of the glory of God.*" God extended me His Grace, and Mercy. He didn't have to let me live nor did He denied me the right to stay; He gave me a chance to make things right with him. I read in a book about certain Biblical characters about, "David, despite being a great ruler, he was also a fornicator and an adulterer. Saul was a disbeliever; Moses was a doubter with a stuttering problem and Jacob was a liar that wrestled with God all night long and wouldn't let go of Him until God promised to bless him; God changed his name from Jacob to Israel. Although, I was a sinner and very disobedient, God granted me unmerited favors."

We are all children of God, despite the fact that we have all sinned over and over and over again, He extends us His grace and mercy for free. And, He never ask anything from us. He wants us to have love in our hearts, and in due time, the love that we planted in our hearts, will manifest into roots and bear fruits.

# "VENGEANCE BELONGS TO GOD."

*Do not take revenge, dear friends, but leave room for God's wrath. For it is written, "Vengeance belongs to me. I will pay them back, declares the Lord."*
*Roman 12:19*

After I got saved and baptized, my marriage and faith were tested. Now, no one never told me that once I gave my heart to God that my life was going to be like living in paradise. My husband became controlling, abusive; mentally and physically. Every time I got pregnant, he cheated on me; he cheated throughout the entire marriage which is why the marriage ended in divorce and sometimes, he wouldn't come home at all. This man was so controlling and jealous that one day we were going somewhere in the car, I forgot where, but while he was driving, he asked me, "What nigga are you trying to see?"

"What?" I said because I had no clue as to what this man was talking about.

"You heard me; what nigga are you trying to see? Why are you wearing your eye glasses in the car?" He said.

"Are you kidding me, you know that these are my prescription eye glasses," I said.

And, the next thing I knew, he hit me so hard in my eye while he was driving. My eye immediately swelled up and turned black, I couldn't see out of my eye for days, I had to walk around with super dark sunglasses on so no one could see my black eye.

This one particular day, my husband knew that I had school and school let out at 10:00 p.m. So, I would leave work and went straight to school. My husband who was never at home, had the audacity to tell to me that morning before going to work, "You better be home before 10:00 p.m."

I turned to him and said, "You know that I go to school after work and school doesn't let out until ten p.m."

"Like I said, you better be home at ten p.m.," he said.

I went to work as usual and after work, I went to school. I am thinking to myself; he knows that I am going to school and he's trying to control me; acting like, he's, my dad. He can come and go when he pleases and some days, he doesn't come home at all. But it's a problem when I want to go to school, now he wants to tell me what time to come home. I stayed at school until the professor let us out and all the time I was thinking, I know he's going to be mad, but I really don't care. I am at home with my sons all the time; sometimes, I feel like a single mom. My mind was thinking about the hell this man put me through, but I made a vow to God, "For better or worse, in sickness and in health, for richer or poorer, till death do we part."

Getting married is making a vow before God to become one in Christ Jesus until death do you part; God holds us to our vows no matter how bad or hard things gets, the only way out is 'til death do you part; unless, adultery is committed, because of the hardness of your heart, God will allow you to divorce; God deals with our hearts. Divorce is not an option in God's eye. God keeps His promises when dealing with us and He expects us to keep our promise. And, the Bible clearly says that, "Marriage is not to be taken lightly."

Although, I married this man that I was not in love with; but only because I had two babies by him out of wedlock, and I wanted to make things right with God; so, I took my marriage vows seriously, divorce was never going to be an option for me. Even though I married him for all the wrong reasons, I had convinced myself that I could grow to love him; besides, I wanted all of my sons to have the same daddy; and not different baby daddies. When we decided to fornicate, to have sex and not married, in God's eyes, we became one and were already married spiritually. And, marriage was only meant to be for one man and one woman to be joined in Holy matrimony, we were never supposed to get divorced; let alone divorcing two, three, four, five, six, seven or eight times.

So, as I am getting closer to my house coming down the street, I looked at the clock and the clock said 10:15 p.m. As I pulled into the driveway and got out of the car and unlock the front door, he was standing right by the door and as soon as I was getting ready to walk in, he grabbed me. He pulled me in the house by my neck, chocking me. I couldn't breathe, I tried to get his hands off of my neck but he became very aggressive and threw me on the floor and started punching me in my face and just went into a rage. He sat on top of me, and started choking me while I was laying on the floor.  I don't remember what happened after that because he was choking me so hard that I blacked out and lost conscious. When I finally woke up from still laying on the floor, I looked at the clock and it was three o'clock in the morning and I was laying on the floor from 10:20 p.m. until three o'clock in the morning; this man tried to kill me. He choked me until I passed out and didn't care if I was dead because he left me on the floor unconscious; while, he was in the bed, sleeping like a baby.

I got to thinking to myself, I am tired of him putting his hands on me.  Just a while ago, he was physical with me and I had gotten up at three a.m. put my kids in the car and drove off really fast, I just wanted to get far away from him as I possibly could.  I had the car running and ran quietly back in the house making sure that he didn't wake up, grabbed one son, put him in the car and ran back in the house and grabbed son number two and after I grabbed son number three, I drove around all morning looking for a shelter to go too.

After I had been gone for two weeks now, sleeping in the car with my three sons who were about two, four and six years old at that time, I was at work calling around trying to find a shelter; thank you Jesus, they finally had an available spot for me and my sons; I was so happy, sleeping and living in a car wasn't easy and I sure wasn't going back home. I was mentally and physically exhausted from living in a car with three small babies; going on two weeks, going to work every day, calling around trying to find a shelter was one of the hardest things I have ever done. No time to get tired now, I had to do what I had to do.

The bad thing about my situation is that I was married, but couldn't go home after work; instead, I am at work trying to find somewhere for my sons and I to sleep for the night.  Sometimes, after picking them up from Day Care, I had to sleep in the car with my babies because all the shelters were full.  I definitely was not going to leave my sons with just anyone, I was scared to leave them at Day Care because of what I went through coming up as a child; being violated by older men. And, that was around the same time the Catholic Priests were messing with those little boys.

I didn't realize that I had brought some of my childhood problems into my marriage, I didn't trust no one, not even my husband; who was my sons dad, in fear of someone violating them. I would be at work and couldn't work because I was at work; crying, and thinking that my sons were at home being violated. I didn't trust the Day Care neither; but, in this case, I had to take them to Day Care because I was not planning on going back home no time soon. So, when I got off of work, I would rush to pick up my sons, take their diapers and underwear off and check their buttocks for any little mark; to make sure, no one was messing with them.

And, when it was starting to get dark, I would look back in the backseat and saw my babies sleeping, their little heads falling everywhere. My heart was breaking for them, I would cry softly because I didn't want to wake them and I could tell they were not comfortable; they were too young to understand what was going on and probably wished that they were at home sleeping comfortable in their own beds. I refused to go back home and put up with the abuse, I didn't want to expose my sons to that kind of life style nor did I want them to grow up thinking that this is how you are supposed to treat a woman.

Finally, the YWCA (a shelter for Women with children) had an opening for me and my sons; the only problem was, they had no beds for us to sleep in. After leaving work, I got my sons and we went to the shelter. It was a really bad situation because it was going on ten p.m. when I arrived there with my sons and they still didn't have any beds for us to sleep in. There were women and children everywhere laying on the floor; waiting for beds. The place was packed to where my sons and I literally had to step over people just to try to find a space for all of us to sleep together. So, as we sat on the floor getting prepared to go to sleep, one of the workers walked over to me and said, "Excuse me Ma'am but is your name Maxine?"

"Yes," I said.

"You have a phone call," she said.

Looking confused and thinking to myself, 'Who knows that I am here, I hope and pray that he didn't track me and the kids down.' As I got the phone and said, "Hello." I immediately recognized the voice on the other end of the phone, it was my sister-in-law and she asked me,

"Maxine, what are you doing? I had been calling around everywhere trying to find you and the boys, I called every shelter and every YWCA that I can think of. Why are you and the boys not at home? Why are you guys in a shelter?"

After explaining to her what happened, she said, "Maxine, I am so sorry that you went through that, I know that's my brother and I am not making any excuses for him but wrong is wrong and he definitely was wrong. I can't have you and the boys sleeping on the floor in a shelter, I want you and the boys to come here to my place, we will talk later and I am not taking no for an answer."

"Okay, but it's late; it's after midnight."

"I don't care what time it is, come over here and I am not going to bed until you and the boys get here," she said.

"Okay, we are on our way." After two more weeks of staying with my sister-in-law, the boys and I went back home; I was tired of running and I wanted them to be able to finally sleep comfortable in their own beds. Now, here I am a couple of weeks later and he is acting crazy and controlling again; being physically abusive. But this time after him being physical with me, I thought out a plan in my head, I premeditated how I was going to kill my husband.

So, my plan was to leave him again but first I was going to super glue his hands to his balls while he was sleeping so, if he wakes up and tried to hit me, he wouldn't be able to. Then, I was going to put four pots of water on the stove making sure they were boiling, good and hot, that I was going to throw all over on him. Then, I was going to get a hammer and bash his head in while he was sleeping; and last but not least, I was going to get the biggest gasoline can that I could buy, fill it up with gasoline and pour it all over him; setting him on fire. I was going to do like the movie, "The Burning Bed."

So, as I made my second attempt to leave my husband, I said in my mind that I was going to get up at two a.m. before he wakes up and carry out my plan. I accidentally slept a little longer than I had anticipated, it was three o'clock in the morning and I quietly got up put the pots on the stove and turned it on, making sure they will be good and hot. I put the super glue in my pocket, went and got my kids quietly out of their beds, making sure not to wake them; I put a blanket over each one's face so they wouldn't wake up nor get wet because it was pouring down raining so hard that morning. I had to try to move as quickly as possible and quietly as I possibly could, I had the car running again. I got the hammers out of the car; I deliberately left the hammers in the car so he wouldn't see them and get suspicious. I ran quietly back in the house making sure that he didn't wake up, grabbed one son, put him in the car and ran back in the house and grabbed son number two and as I ran in and grabbed son number three to put him in the car, a police car with two Police Officers in it was driving down the street. They saw me carrying child number three in my arms out of the house; in the rain. They stopped in front of my house, got out of the car and walked up to me and asked me what was I doing outside in the rain with a child in a blanket, putting him in a running car with two other babies already in the car.

"I am going to kill my husband," I said.

They looked at one another and said to one another, "We are going inside to check this out." They helped me put the babies back in the house and immediately saw all of the evidence and looked at one another and said, "She wasn't lying."

"Where's your husband at?" They asked.

"He's in the bedroom, still in the bed sleeping," I said. They turned and looked at one another again in disbelief. They help me put the babies back in their beds and went into my bedroom, turned on the light and woke him up. They told him to put some clothes on because he only had on his boxers and no shirt. As they stood there and waited for him to finish putting on his clothes, they asked him to turn around and put his hands around his back, then they handcuffed him.

Then they said to him, "Sir, we are placing you under arrest."

"Why?" He asked.

"Trust us, this is for your own good. We are trying to save your life," they said.

They put him in the back of the police car and came back inside the house to talk to me, they asked me what happened and what was going on. I explained everything to them about the physical abuse and they told me that they were going to put him in a holding cell for

48 hours (two days) so, I can decide what I was going to do and find somewhere else for me and my sons to go. They advised me that I was a woman with small children, so he should be the one leaving; or, I can stay here and if I stay, they advised me to change the locks to the doors; so, he couldn't get back in. They said he would have to have a key to get back in the house and if the locks are changed, he can't get back in and since he can't get back in, he would have to come through a window and if he comes in through a window, call us and we will be back out to arrest him for breaking and entering; then we can hold him longer, for a breaking and entering.

So, after he got out, we separated for a while and months later, he came back home. Soon after that, he became physical again; angry and mad because I went to school and came home after ten p.m.; fifteen minutes after his curfew that he gave me, choking me until I blacked out and him probably hoping that he had killed me this time, didn't sit well with me at all. So once again, I premeditated his death. I said to myself, "He is not going to put his hands on me not one more time, this time I am going to kill him. I am going to super glue his hands to his balls, then I am going to pour hot water on him, then I am going to bash his head in with a hammer and then I am going to do the burning bed on him, I am going to set him on fire. Everybody has a breaking point, and I've reached my breaking point; my dad never put his hands on me and he's not going to put his hands on me ever again."

All of a sudden, this voice appeared out of nowhere, it said, *"Vengeance is mine."* As I got up off of the floor, looking around trying to see where the voice came from because everyone including my husband was in the bed sound asleep. I didn't see anyone; so, I proceeded with my premeditation of how I was going to kill him, I was thinking to myself, 'no one is going to stop me this time, I reached my breaking point.'

The voice said again, *"Vengeance is mine, I will repay."*

Finally, I realized that was God speaking to me. So, I answered God back in an angry voice and said, "God, I know you said, "Vengeance is yours," but you are taking too long. I want him dead and I want him dead now." God never said anything back to me after that, and I went to bed and said, "I am going to get up at three a.m. and carry out my plans."

Unfortunately, I had overslept and it was seven o'clock in the morning and the light that was shining so bright through the windows woke me up, I got so angry at myself for not waking up at three a.m. I couldn't set the alarm because I didn't want to wake him; so, I figured, I might as well get up and fix the kids their breakfast. All of a sudden, I had trouble moving. My entire left side was feeling tingling, I was weak and had trouble getting out of bed. I had to pick my left leg and arm up because they fell asleep on me. I asked my husband to help me get out of bed. "Max, there's nothing wrong with you," he said.

So, after a while, I finally was able to get myself out of the bed and I noticed that as I was walking, my left side was getting numbed and more numbed. I started to panic and decided to go to the hospital to see what was wrong with me, as I finally made it down the stairs on the front porch and to my car, I noticed that I had two flat tires. As I stood there in disbelief, my neighbor next door saw me standing there looking down, asked me what's wrong. I told him that I wasn't feeling well and were trying to go to the hospital, but I noticed that I had two flat tires.

"You look okay to me. But I'll change your tires for you so you can be on your way," he said. As I stood there waiting for him to finish changing my flat tires, I noticed that my left side was getting worse and I knew then that I wasn't going to make it to the hospital, it was too far away. So, after he finished changing my tires, I decided to drive over to my mama's house which was only six blocks away and asked her to drive me to the hospital.

After my mom and I made it to the hospital, we went through Emergency and they immediately admitted me and put me in a room. While I was in my room laying in the bed, a Nurse was standing by my bed hooking me up to everything, I remember hearing my mother and the doctor standing right outside my room, discussing me. I heard the doctor say after running a lot of tests, he was explaining the results to her.

"There is a spot on her right brain, the right brain is not communicating with the left side of her brain. There is something wrong with her brain," he said.

"You got that right when you said that there is something wrong with her brain, the girl has always been crazy," I heard my mother say to the doctor. I got so mad and wanted to get out of the bed and let my mother have a few good words because I had never disrespected my mother; I was angry at her for saying something like that to the doctor about me; luckily for her, I was paralyzed and couldn't get out of the bed.

I turned to the Nurse upset and angry after hearing what my mother had said to the doctor, "Nurse, I don't want no visitors, and no TV. Can you please turn the TV off?"

"Honey, your TV is not on," she said.

"Yes, it is. Turn it off," I said.

She turned and looked over at the TV and said, "No Honey, your TV is not on."

I turned and looked at the TV and my mouth felled wide open as I stared at the TV, I realize that it was God showing me myself, of every sin that I committed; most of the sins I recognized and others, I didn't. It was shocking, hurtful and shameful watching myself on TV; committing all kinds of sins.

"Oh my God, that's me," I said out loud.

The Nurse turned to me and said, "What's wrong?"

I pointed to the TV and said, "That's me."

When she turned and looked at the TV, God spoke to me and said, "Repent!"

Then He said it a second time, "Repent!"

"Okay! Okay! I repent," I said.

The Nurse quickly ran out of the room; while she was not in the room, God spoke to me again and said, "I want you to say this prayer for three days and on the third day, you shall be healed; you shall walk again."

The nurse walked back in my room with four Doctors and two Psychiatrists, they all stood at the foot of my bed looking at me.

"We could strap her down, but she's paralyzed; so, it's no point. She can't walk anyway," one of the Psychiatrists said.

"Mrs. Wheeler, we understand that you are seeing things and hearing voices," said the other Psychiatrists.

"No," I said. "That was God showing me myself on TV and talking to me. He told me to repent and to say this prayer for three days and I shall be healed; I shall walk again."

"You are never going to walk again; you had a stroke in your sleep. The type of stroke that you had, no one never recovers from it," said the Doctor.

"God told me to say this prayer for three days and on the third day, I shall be healed; I shall walk again," I said.

So, as I watched the four Doctors and two Psychiatrists pulled out their notepads getting ready to write something down, one Doctor said to me, "What is this prayer that God told you to say?"

As I listen for a moment for God to speak to me, all four doctors and the two psychiatrists were standing there staring at me, waiting for me to tell them the prayer.

"God won't tell me what the prayer is," I said.

"Well, if God is really talking to you, then we will find out. We are going to leave and come back in three days, we want to see you get up out of that bed and walk," one of the doctors said as they all turned and left out of my room, including the Nurse.

After everyone left out of the room, God spoke to me; He told me the prayer to say for three days. After everyone had left out of my room and God stopped talking to me, I noticed my health got worse. I was completely paralyzed, I couldn't feel my tongue, I couldn't see out of my left eye, the left side of my face was twisted so my speech was slurred and I could barely talk; I had no feelings in my left foot, hand or arm. While sitting in my bed, someone came in my room and put a big and bright, orange banner over my bed that said, 'NOTHING BY MOUTH.'

I had to get my food through a tube injected in my arm; every day, they brought me little toys and gadgets to play with, but I couldn't lift them; let alone hold a piece of paper. For three days, I did exactly what God told me to do; I said the prayers for three days, all day. I didn't worry about anything nor did I doubt God, I was truly happy on the inside that God was going to heal me and make me to walk again.

Day three: The four doctor's and the two psychiatrists came into my bedroom at five a.m. I haven't seen them nor talked to any of them since they left out of my room three days ago. They woke me up, "Mrs. Wheeler, wake up. This is the third day, you said that your God told you that He was going to heal you and that you were going to walk again. We want to see you get out of that bed and walk." They handed me a walker, a cane, and a wheelchair to assist me.

"I don't need any of those things, God is going to heal me," I said to them.

"Do you want to hold onto my arm for support?" asked one of the doctors.

"No!" I said.

Deep down in my spirit, I started talking to God. "God, you told me that You were going to heal me on the third day; well, today is the third day and I still can't feel my left side, I still can't walk. I am trusting you God to heal me; so, I am about to get up out of this bed and walk, it's just you and me God," I said as I was struggling trying to get up out of the bed; using my right hand to pick up my left leg, so I can get out of the bed. Moments later, I finally got out of the bed, holding onto the wall, while noticing that everyone was staring at me.

Minutes later, I finally made my way slowly to the door, while dragging my left leg like a zombie. "We want to see you walk all the way down to the end of the hallway," said one of the doctors. I looked down the hallway, it was the longest hallway that I had ever seen.

"Okay God, here I go. I am trusting You; it's just me and you, so please don't let me down," I said as I proceeded to drag myself down the hallway.

"No, don't hold onto the wall," I heard one of the doctor's say.

I kept my mind on God as I dragged myself down that long hallway; finally, I made it all the way down to the end of the hallway.

"Now, turn around and come back," said one of the doctors.

As I proceeded to turn around, I could feel my left foot, then my left hand, then my tongue; the more I walked, the more I could feel my body. I even felt the left side of my face and tongue. I yelled to the four doctors and the two Psychiatrists, "I can feel my feet, and my hand; I can feel my entire left side."

By the time I got back to my room, I was immediately healed and no longer dragged myself down that long hallway; I was completely healed, walking normal and talking normal. My face was no longer twisted, and my speech was normal, it was as if nothing never happened to me. God kept his word, He healed me on the third day, just like He said.

Once in my room, the four doctors and two psychiatrists were all amazed. They re-examine me and found me to be in perfect health.

"Your God is truly your God, He healed you. You are a miracle patient; we are discharging you. You are free to go home." The doctor told the Nurse that I can order me something to eat, on a regular full diet and arrange for someone to pick me up, because there was no need to keep me in the hospital and they removed that big, bright, and orange banner from over my bed that said, 'NOTHING BY MOUTH.

Once back in my room, I said, "I want to keep saying that prayer," but I couldn't remember it anymore; God had erased it from my memory…

# *TESTIMONY #4:*
# "THE SEVENTH COMMANDMENT."

*"Thou shall not commit adultery." Exodus 20 (KJV)*

One day, I heard my husband on the phone speaking with someone, so I eased the phone off of the hook and listened to his conversation; he was talking to one of his cousins.

"Man, you pay all the bills in the house, you should come home whenever you want. Man, snatch that b**ch by her hair and beat the sh*t out of her," I heard his cousin say.

"Man, I come and go as I please; I always keep me a spare tire," I heard my husband say.

"Why don't you come over here and beat my a**, b**ch? I will kill you both," I said as I interrupted their conversation.

Once my husband and his cousin got off the phone, my husband and I had a physical fight. He told me that he was going to make my life a living hell and how he was going to make me miscarry. I was five months pregnant; with my youngest son, when he left and was gone for months.

One day unexpectedly, I came home with my two other sons; I pulled up in the driveway and saw his car and the side window up, so I sat in the car with my two sons, one and three years old. I called the police and waited for them to arrive before going in the house.

The police officers arrived, and we all walked in the house together, only to find my husband in the house. They asked him for his ID and asked him did he live here; he told them that he did. They asked him did he have a key and he told them 'No.' Then they asked him how did he get in the house without a key. He told them that he was gone for a while and while he was gone, I had the locks changed; so, he had to climb through the side window to get in; which, was still up.

I figured that his girlfriend was hiding somewhere in my house and she must have planned on sleeping over because I saw an overnight bag, with rollers and a night gown in it, on my sofa.

While the police officers were talking to him, "I noticed that my sons were standing in the door of my husband and I bedroom, looking up. I had already seen her overnight bag, along with rollers and a night gown that I knew didn't belong to me.

"He has his girlfriend in my house somewhere because her stuff is on my sofa," I said to the Police Officers. The Police Officers looked at another as I walked in our bedroom to find out what it was that my sons were looking up at; she was hiding on the side of the wall, trying to shhh my sons.

"Officers, here she is; hiding in my bedroom," I said.

The Police Officers came back in the bedroom and said, 'Ma'am, you are going to have to get your belongings and leave." And, they then went back to my husband and told him that they were placing him under arrest. They told him to turn around, put his hands behind his back, placed handcuffs on him, and took him down to the police station.

After I had my son, my husband didn't stop cheating. So, I decided to get even with him, and besides, the Bible said that grounds for divorce was due to adultery only; so, I wanted to commit adultery just to get out of this marriage; even though, I tried to take my marriage vows seriously, he didn't and I no longer wanted to be married to someone who didn't want to be married to me. So, I plotted how I wanted him to come home from work and catch me in bed with another man; since I had walked in on him one day coming home only to find him in bed with a girl and they had sexual intercourse because the evidence was all over the sheets in the bed that he tried to cover up with a towel; instead, of washing them because he wanted me to see the evidence all over the bed.

So, I decided to get even; an eye for an eye. I had a long-time friend since the ninth grade come over, who had a crush on me for years; so, I called him over just when I knew that my husband would be walking through the door. He called and told me that he was working over, I wanted him to catch me in the act.

After three failed years of plotting to get even with my husband; committing adultery, and wanting him to come home and catch me in the act; I finally gave up. I repented and ask God to forgive me because I spent the first three years plotting to get even with my husband, and I spent the last twelve years being faithful and he never stopped cheating. I didn't gain any thing by doing what I did, I felt dirty and nasty. I couldn't believe that I had stooped down to his level and degraded myself, and to make sure that I didn't hurt God again or degrade myself, I walked around with The Ten Commandments on a piece of paper that I kept with me, trying to make sure that I did not break not one of them.

*James 2:10 – 11 (ERV) says, "You might follow all of God's law. But if you fail to obey only one command, you are guilty of breaking all the commands in that law. 11. God said, "Don't commit adultery." The same God also said, "Don't kill." So, if you don't commit adultery, but you kill someone, you are guilty of breaking all of God's law.*

*Hebrews 13:4*

*"Marriage should be honored by all, and the marriage bed kept pure, for God will judge the adulterer and all the sexually immoral.*

May God have mercy on all of our souls.

One day, while the kids and I were at church, he was out there whoring around. One of my sons asked me, "Mommy, how come daddy never go to church with us?"

I regret to this day the bad answer that I gave my son. I said, "I don't know why daddy doesn't go to church with us, why don't you ask your dad why he doesn't go with us."

"Dad, why don't you go to church with us?" my son asked him.

"Son, when I was little, I had to go; now that I am grown, I don't have to go and y'all don't have to go neither."

From that day forward, he would get up early every Sunday morning, wanting to pick a fight with me, stood by the side door; because we only used our side door and said, "You can go to church but you're not taking the boys with you."

So, I politely went in the bathroom and quietly dialed 911.

"9-1-1 what's your emergency?" the operator asked.

"My husband just jumped on me," I said.

"Are you in a safe place?" She asked.

"I locked myself in the bathroom. Please hurry, I have small kids in the house," I  said.

"Okay, a police car has been dispatched and is on the way," she said.

The Police showed up, put him in handcuffs and took him down to the Police Station, me and my sons went onto church as if nothing happened.  Sadly, to say, this was my every Sunday situation.  Police being called, him being hauled off to jail and my sons and I went to church as if nothing happened.  He eventually caught on to what was going to happen to him if he tried to stop me from taking my sons to church and had his work scheduled changed to where he worked every Sunday from then on out and the Police no longer had to come back out every Sunday morning.

But then I started noticing how he would treat and talk to my oldest son; who was only six years old. "Get away from your mama, stop sitting next to her; you are going to grow up and be gay," he would say.

"He can sit next to me! He doesn't have to move!" I said.

Then he wouldn't call him by his name; which is the same name as his, but would say, "That nigga this or that nigga that."

"Who are you calling a nigga? Because as I recall, every one of my sons have a name," I said.

"I'm talking about the nigga that is sitting next to you," he said.

"His name is the same as yours and I suggest that you call him by his name, nigga," I said.

I was so hurt to hear him call my son, six years old, out of his name.  He is our first-born son, and just the thought of me naming him after him; made my blood boil.  I went outside to catch my breath and so my son wouldn't see me crying.  As I was standing by the fence, I prayed to God. "God, why does this man hate my son so bad?"

*"Because you breast fed,"* said God.

Wow! God reminded me of the day that I gave birth to my son, our first-born son, who at the time were just two days old. This man came up to the hospital, walked in my room while I was breast feeding him and immediately got mad and said, "I don't want no other nigga sucking your breast."

"You can leave because you will never suck my breasts," I said as I had him put out of my room. Who calls a two-day old baby a nigga? He had continued to call him that until I put my feet down and stopped him from calling my son out of his name. Every time, he called my son a nigga, I called him a nigga.

# "DON'T FORGET TO TELL GOD, 'THANK YOU.'"

*Luke 17:11-19; (KJV) 11. "And it came to pass, as he went to Jerusalem, that he passed through the midst of Samaria and Galilee. 12. And as he entered into a certain village, there met him ten men that were lepers, which stood afar off. 13. And they lifted up their voices, and said, Jesus, Master, have mercy on us. 14. And when he saw them, he said unto them, Go shew yourselves unto the priests. And it came to pass that, as they went, they were cleansed. 15. And one of them, when he saw that he was healed, turned back, and with a loud voice glorified God. 16. And fell down on his face at his feet, giving him thanks: and he was a Samaritan. 17. And Jesus answering said, Were there not ten cleansed? But where are the nine? 18. There are not found that returned to give glory to God, save this stranger. 19. And he said unto him, Arise, go thy way: thy faith hath made thee whole."*

One day, after coming home from work, the landlord came over to the house that we were living in with his oldest brother and said that she never knew that we were living in her house, she had rented it out to my brother-in-law. He was driving a milk truck at the time, which were my husband's family-owned business; delivering dairy products to over forty stores. So, by him never being home, he told us that we can live there with him. The landlord after finding out that we were staying in her house, with small children decided to raise our rent every three months, because she said, "I never wanted to rent to tenants with small children and because I don't want them tearing my house up." Needless to say, one day while I was at work, my sons called me and said, "Mommy, you are going to be so proud of us when you get home, we decorated the house for you."

"Where's your dad?" I asked.

"He's asleep on the couch," they said.

After getting home from work and seeing the house and what the kids had done, my mouth felled wide open. They had not only decorated the house but took some black crayons and had drawn big black stars all over the walls, they had broken the soap dish off of the bathtub, they had taken my Maxi Pads, took the tape off of the back of the Maxi pads and stuck them on the walls and had rearranged all of my furniture; putting my kitchen chairs in the living room, and some of the living room furniture in the kitchen. All I could think of was, if the landlord were to come over right now, she will definitely put us out; considering, she didn't want us living there in the first place.

So, after the kids went to bed that night, I went in the living room, got down on my knees and prayed. I asked God for a three-bedroom, ranch style house, with a formal dining room, a full basement, and a two-car garage. A week later, my husband came home and said, "Max, I found us a house." I was so excited, we met with the Real Estate Agent, signed all of the papers and he handed us the keys to the house. I will never forget what the owner of the house said to the Realtor, "They are just babies, I have kids older than them. I want to sell my house to someone who is going to take care of my house."

My husband said, "These babies wants to buy your house and you are going to lose it anyway, you owe back taxes and your mortgage is behind. We are willing to buy your house, catch up your back taxes and we will pay your past due mortgage as well." She couldn't afford to pay the back taxes on the house which were over $8,000 back from eight years ago and she only got Social Security, her mortgage on the house were only $125 a month and she couldn't afford to pay that as well.

She immediately asked, "Where do I sign?" After leaving from the Realtor, and him giving us the keys to the house, immediately I asked my sister-in-law the next day to go with me to see the house; my husband had seen the house, I haven't. As we pulled up to this vacant house that wasn't fit for anyone to live in, there was no driveway; we had to drive up on the grass, which was taller than the porch. The roof was caving in, the windows were shot and the garage door was falling off the hinges with a lot of old car parts inside the garage and in the alley. Once we made our way inside, it was almost as bad as the outside; it smelled awful. You can tell that no one had lived in the house for a while and cats were living up in the house, because when we drove up to the house, cats were everywhere; outside by the side door.

There was this dirty royal blue carpet on the floor, throughout the entire house. As we entered the living room, I wanted to cry and my sister-in-law knew that I was embarrassed and hurt, turned to me and said, "It's going to be okay, Max. You can always fix it up the way you want." I was just in total disbelief and shocked that my husband would purchase this ugly, ran down house for us and the kids; this was the ugliest, abandoned house that I had ever seen.

Before moving into the house, the first thing I did was put blinds up in every room, my husband brought all new appliances; stove, refrigerator, washer, dryer and a floor model 36-inch TV. When I came home from work, my husband immediately went to working on the house, he had men putting in a brand-new driveway, a new roof on the house and had new windows coming within the week or so. He had a new garage door put on the garage and there was a big tree stump in the front yard; along with, two big old trees on the curb but the big tree stump in the front yard was gone. When I asked what happened to the tree stump that was in the middle of the front yard, he said, "Him and the boys pulled it up." The grass was cut and he had installed new front and side doors. One of his friends that we had went to school with were in the alley, cutting the grass with a weed wacker because the grass was too tall to cut with a lawn mower; and, he removed the old car parts out of the garage and alley. The house was finally coming together and was now looking like a home. I was still embarrassed to have anyone come over because the kitchen still needed work done to it. So, I decided to paint the entire kitchen myself; there were so many coats of paint on the wall that it was hard to cover up the old layers of paint that was underneath it. We paid the house off in two years, and the former owner of the house was so happy with us that she said that she was in the neighborhood and wanted to stop and see the inside of the house because we had fixed the outside up really nice.

She was so happy once she came inside and saw all the work that we had done inside the house. "I almost didn't recognize the house when I was coming down the street; so, I had to stop so I could see the inside. Baby, y'all ready did a good job fixing up the house, y'all are the best tenants that I ever had, y'all always paid your mortgage on time and paid extra, giving me a bonus at Christmas time. I didn't have to remind y'all when the Mortgage was due; your husband, every first of the month drove over to me and handed me the money. I really appreciate you and your husband," she said. We paid the house off in two years on land contract, we didn't have any credit because we saved our money and paid for everything in cash, which is why, my husband chose to go with land contract; opposed to getting a mortgage.

Four years later, I was sitting in my dining room, writing. This was my very first time writing a book and my husband and the boys were gone to a baseball game, my oldest son had won four tickets over the radio to go to the Detroit Lions game; so, I was home alone having me some me time. I was so into my writing when suddenly, God spoke to me.

*"Four years ago, you asked me for a three-bedroom, ranch style house with a formal dining room, a full basement, and a two-car garage,"* he said back to me verbatim.

"Yes," I said.

*"And, you never once said 'thank you,"* said God.

# "GOD'S WORDS ARE SHARPER THAN A TWO-EDGED SWORD."

*Hebrews 4:12 (NLT) says, "For the word of God is alive and powerful. It is sharper than any two-edged sword, piercing to the division of soul and of spirit, of joints and of marrow, and discerning the thoughts and intentions of the heart."*

After God finished speaking those words to me, I almost fell out of the chair while sitting at the dining room table, God's words pierced through my heart. I grabbed my chest; I was in so much excruciating pain. I felt hurt, ashamed, and embarrassed, because I did asked God for a three-bedroom, ranch style house with a formal dining room, a full basement, and a two-car garage. And, because I was so focused on the outer appearance of the house, I forgot about my blessing. Now here I am, appearing unthankful, ungrateful, and unappreciative because now that I am living in my nice, warm, cozy and beautiful home, enjoying every room in the house, it took God four years later to remind me of how ungrateful, and how unappreciative I was; I asked, I received and I never once said 'thank you.'

When God's words pierced through my heart, it was almost like someone had shot me with a bow and arrow, my heart almost stopped. I can't even explain the pain because it was that excruciating; I cried uncontrollably, but I knew that I had to ask for His forgiveness. Twenty-six years after still living in that house, we still had the same original appliances: stove, refrigerator, washer, dryer that never broke down; never gave us any problems.

Praise be to God, Glory Hallelujah, thank you Jesus. For your mercy endures forever, I love You Heavenly Father God, and I thank You for everything, and for all things. Lord, Father God, you are my heart and I love you; I can't say sorry enough but I am truly sorry for the way that I hurt you. You mean the world to me; you are my everything. I appreciate you and I don't take you for granted nor any of my blessings for granted in Jesus' name. Amen.

*When you pray and ask God for anything, thank Him in advance or as soon as you get finish praying, because He is waiting to hear you say, 'thank you.'*

# "THE SIXTH COMMANDMENT."

## *THOU SHALL NOT KILL – EXODUS 20 (KJV)*

While still living at the old house before we moved, my husband's cousin and his wife came over to visit and he was telling me how I can become sterile without having my tubes tied. I already have two kids and didn't want anymore because every time I became pregnant, I had to fight with my husband. After we had our first son; at 21 years old, I got pregnant and we weren't married at the time but living together. So, after I got pregnant again, immediately after my first son, he told me that he didn't want any more children and that his dad was going to kill him and he told me to get rid of it. He took me down to the abortion clinic and I aborted my baby. I cried, because I didn't want to get rid of my baby. I hated myself for killing a human being, listening to a man. How stupid and hurt that made me feel, I felt less than a woman; incomplete.

Soon after that, I became pregnant again and my baby daddy said the same thing again, he told me to get rid of it. So, he took me down to the abortion clinic to abort my unborn child, which is my second son. He dropped me off and told me to call him after I had the abortion so he can come and pick me up. I went inside, signed in and went to the back of the room and sat down. Sadly, to say, the room was almost filled up; a lot of women sitting in the waiting room, alone; waiting to abort their unborn child. I had noticed that when my baby daddy, because we weren't married at the time, had dropped me off, that it was only men that were dropping off the women; cowardly sitting in their cars, outside of the building too embarrassed and/or too ashamed to come inside with the women; they left and came back to pick up the women after the mission was completed. I did not see one man sitting inside the abortion clinic with the women, so as I took my seat in the back of the room, it took a long time for my name to be called. Finally, it was my turn, I heard my name being called.

"Maxine."

"Maxine."

"Maxine," I heard the lady say. I just sat in my chair and never said a word, I don't know how she knew me but she walked over to me and said, "Are you Maxine?"

"Yes," I said.

She looked in my eyes and said, "You don't want to do this?"

"No, I don't," I said.

"Honey, that is your body. If you don't want to do this, then don't. I tell you what, why don't you sleep for about two hours and then I will come and wake you up, and then you can call your ride to come and pick you up," she said to me.

"Okay," I said. After two hours, she came and woke me up, I called my baby daddy to come and pick me up.

"Max, you had the abortion already?" he asked.

"Yes," I said.

"Okay, I will be right there," he said. He came and picked me up, he smiled all the way home. I smiled all the way home too. Months later, my stomach was beginning to show and he said to me, "Max, I thought you said that you had an abortion?"

"No, I did not get an abortion. I am not getting rid of my baby for you. Since you don't want any more kids, how about you cut it off and don't touch me again. As a matter of fact, let me do the Lorena Bobbitt on you and cut it off for you," I said.

"My dad is going to kill me," he said.

"You are right, he is going to kill you. He's not my dad so I am not worried about him putting his hands on me," I said.

The next thing I knew, he had hit me and we starting fighting, him throwing me up against the wall and chocking me. He threw me on the floor and started punching me in the face and stomach trying to make me miscarry. Even before, I found out that I was pregnant and before he took me down to the abortion clinic to get an abortion, I was on birth control pills and was still having my menstrual cycle. I was pregnant and didn't even know it; he knew every time I was pregnant, because he had all the morning sickness, and the cravings; I didn't have any of the symptoms and I never knew that I was pregnant until he asked me was I pregnant. I had the same problems with all of my pregnancies; except, I wasn't on birth control pills with my first born. All of my pregnancy tests would come back 'negative,' even after I had gone to the doctor and them doing blood work, the tests were still negative up until I was five months pregnant and big as a house; and, finally getting a positive reading. The doctor said, "I can see that you are definitely pregnant, but your body isn't producing any pregnancy hormones. You need to go home, put your feet up because you are threatening a miscarriage." I thought that I was on my menstrual; one, because I never stopped having a period and two, I was having a period while at the doctor's office.

So, when my husband's cousin and his wife came over a year later after having my second child and because I didn't want any more children by my husband, I listened to him and thought of the ideal of me doing an experiment to become fertile sounded like a really good idea.

He told me to get a glass and filled it up with water and put it in the microwave, I forgot how many minutes, but to make sure that I stand in front of the microwave, and put my stomach all the way up against the microwave, turn it on, on high and I will become sterile. I waited until after he left and I did exactly like he told me to do, and the next thing I knew, a shock went through my body. All I heard was zzzzzzz, zzzzzzz, zzzzzzz, like an electric shock going through my body.

Something was in the house because all of a sudden, something picked me up by my neck; I remember looking down and saw my feet dangling about a foot or two off of the ground, it had body slammed me into a wall, in the next room and held me up in the air for about a minute or two; it never said not one word to me and when it finally let me go, I fell to the floor; I was so scared because I was the only one in the house. I was in so much pain, I couldn't walk; I crawled into my bedroom and laid in the bed for two days; in excruciating pain. I called the doctor and asked to be checked out because my back was hurting so bad that I couldn't move, let alone walk; I thought that my back was broke.

After the third day of lying-in the bed, I finally went to the doctor for him to examine me. After running lots of tests, the doctor told me that I was pregnant. I tried to explain to the doctor what had happened and he told me that I was pregnant and the good news was, the baby was good; no harm was done to the baby at all. I was the only one that was having back and body pains. Whatever it was, it knew that I was pregnant and was protecting God's child; I was trying to abort another one of God's creation, without even knowing that I was already pregnant. My youngest son, when he was older, I told him about the story about the microwave, when I was pregnant with him and didn't even know it; to this day, he tells everybody that he was a microwave baby. I can truly say that he was the best child ever; never talked back, never gave me any problems, very mannerable and a little gentleman. He was truly a blessing to me; even though, God blessed me with three good sons.

# "THE SECOND COMMANDMENT."

*"Thou shalt not make unto thee any graven image." – Exodus20 (KJV)*

One day, while I was laid off from my job, I went to visit my aunt in Indiana. Every year they have what they call a May Fair in Alabama, so we drove there for that. While we were there, I saw this drawing of a black Jesus. I had to have this picture; after all, where else can you find such a beautiful masterpiece; I had never seen a picture of a black Jesus before. I thought to myself, 'Wow! A black Jesus. Whenever anyone come over to my house, they will be at awe seeing this picture.' Needless to say, I bought the picture and put it in my car; way in the very back seat of the car making sure that nothing touched it.

As me, my aunt and her daughter left Alabama to drive back to Indiana and we made it to her house, while they were getting their bags and luggage out of the back of the car, I noticed that the glass frame of the black Jesus was cracked. I said to my Auntie, "How did the glass of the picture get broke?" I asked them to not put anything near or close to the picture because I didn't want anything to happen to the picture.

My aunt said to me, "We didn't put anything by your picture, we made sure of that. We knew how you were about that picture; we don't know how it got broke." I was upset that the glass picture frame of my black Jesus was broke and said that I will have to take it to a hardware store to have the glass replaced. So, as they unpacked, I headed back to Michigan, a four-hour drive by myself before it got too dark. I made it home in five hours because construction was so bad and I had to do a lot of detouring.

After making it home, I hurried up to get the picture of the black Jesus out of the back of my car. Now, this time it was only my stuff in the back of the car and I made sure nothing was touching the picture or near it. When I opened the back door and not only seen the glass of the picture broken but it was shattered to pieces, I was so hurt. I'm thinking to myself, 'How did this happened considering nothing was in the back seat except this picture.' I put the picture in the house, in the living room and said to myself, "I will take it to the Hardware store and have the glass replaced." I told my sons to not mess with the picture nor put anything near it, as I was trying to figure out where I wanted to hang the picture so everyone can see it whenever they come over; I sat down on the couch and was staring at the beautiful art that someone had drawn.

When out of nowhere God spoke to me and said, *"Do not make me a graven image."*

Now, on this particular day, no one was at home but me so I put the picture down on the floor and ran out of the living room. Every time, I went in the living room, I heard God's voice say, *"Do not make me a graven image."* I was literally shaking and scared out of my mind. I stopped going into the living room, and whenever I came in the house, I ran pass the living room as fast as I could to keep from hearing God's voice.

After a couple of months of not going into the living room and not hearing God's voice, I decided to go in the living room and look at the picture again. *"Do not make me a graven image,"* God said to me again.

I became so afraid that I was left with only one choice, and that was to get that picture out of my house. So, I took the picture outside and threw it in the garbage can; finally, I had a piece of mind and was able to go back into the living room without hearing God's voice regarding that picture.

# "THE FIRST COMMANDMENT."

*"Thou shalt have no other gods before me." Exodus 20 (KJV)*

One day, while sitting in church and out of nowhere I heard God's voice,

*"I am going to take your son, Wardell's life."*

My heart sunk, I was so scared; I immediately panic, as this was my first-born son. I was crying so hard on the inside, scared and nervous. I started begging and pleading with God in my spirit, "Lord, please, please, I am begging you, I am asking you to please do not take his life. I don't know what he'd done, but please spare him his life. Lord, I promised you that whatever he did, it won't happen again. Please! Please, Lord, I am begging you to not take his life. Lord, what did he do?" I cried out to God from my heart; He never answered me back.

As I am looking around in the sanctuary, I noticed that my son, Wardell, was not sitting with me and my other two sons; I became very worried as I was waiting to hear back from God. I thought to myself, 'He's in the Men's bathroom.' I got up and left the sanctuary and stood outside of the door of the men's bathroom, waiting for my son, Wardell, to come out. While I was standing there waiting for a while, I saw him walking in the front door of the church.

I was so angry, I walked over to him and said, "Wardell, I thought you were in the Men's bathroom, where were you?"

"I went to get my fishes some feeder fish, they have nothing to eat; I am out of food," he said.

"So, you mean to tell me, that you left God's house to go and find food for your fishes?"

"Mom, I don't have no food for my fishes."

"I don't care, you don't leave church. That could have waited and I didn't know you took my car keys; give me my car keys, I'll deal with you later after we get home," I said.

Once we got home, my sister called me and I told her about my son taking my keys and leaving church to find his fishes some feeder food. She said to me, "Girl, you didn't know that? He's been doing that for a while, he calls me just about every Sunday and say, 'Auntie, you know what I am doing? No, what are you doing?" she asked.

"I am driving around in my mama's car," he said.

"Boy, your mama is going to get you," she said.

"No, she's not. I am going to get my fishes some feeder food. So, I thought you knew that he had your car keys and was driving around in your car, looking for food for his fishes," she said. I was boiling, steaming, hot mad.

Once, at home, I explained to him the danger of leaving God's house to go and find his fishes some food. "Wardell," I said. "God is a jealous God," He said, 'have no other gods before me.' You made those fishes your god, every time I ask you to do something, you tell me to 'wait, I have to feed my fishes.' You have brought a curse on this house by putting those fishes first before everything and everyone, I will be damned if I am going to allow you or any of my sons to bring a curse on this house."

"Mom, I went to about four different Fish stores to find feeder fishes and nobody had any, this one store told me that they should be getting some feeder fish in on Wednesday," he said. Wardell went every day after school for three days trying to find feeder fish (gold fishes) for his Green Terror fishes. Wednesday, three days later, he finally found feeder fishes for his Green Terrors. The way those Green Terrors ripped those poor little gold fishes apart, was horrible; he would call his friend over to watch the Green Terrors eat the gold fishes, as if, they were at a movie; all they needed was some popcorn, those poor gold fishes did not stand a chance.

It must have been about 30 gold fishes and six Green Terrors; those gold fishes were all in one corner of the fish tank afraid for their lives; they knew they were dinner. Needless to say, the Green Terrors had eaten all of the gold fishes. The gold fishes, obviously, God caused them to have a disease. So, when the Green Terrors ate them, they immediately turned green, curled up and died; except this one fish, he floated up to the top of the fish tank after he died, it appears to be looking straight up to heaven in the fish tank as to say, 'God did it.' My son, Wardell, was so hurt; I couldn't wait for Sunday to get here, hoping that they had Testimonial Service; so, that I could tell my Testimony.

Bless GOD! God is so good! He allowed the church to have Testimonial Services today; I couldn't wait to tell the church how good God is and what He has done. One of the Deacons in the church stood up and asked if anyone had a Testimony that they would like to share with the Church; now, they don't always have Testimony Services every Sunday; but Glory be to God, thank you Jesus. God is so good! I immediately stood up and said, "Yes, I do."

Now, everybody in the church knows when you see me, you see all three of my sons with me. Church wasn't as crowded that day because it was an afternoon church service, but it was enough people there to hear my Testimony. And, boy oh boy, was I about to give them an ear full. As, I stood up, I begin telling my Testimony to the church, "Church, my son, Wardell, would take my car keys every Sunday, leaving church to go and find his Green Terror fishes some food. Needless to say, three days later, he finally found some food for his Green Terrors. Now, when he fed the feeder fishes to his fishes, what he didn't know is that God caused those feeder fishes to have a disease. So, when the Green Terrors ate the feeder fishes, they immediately turned green, curled up and died. One of the fishes had floated straight to the top, and we all know that fishes don't float to the top of the fish tank, they sink to the bottom of it; but this particular fish, floated straight up to the top; looking straight up to heaven as if to say, 'God did it," I said.

When I thought about how good God is, how he spared my son's life and killed the fishes instead, I got happy. I started shouting, "Glory! Hallelujah! Isn't God good! Won't He do it, thank you, Jesus!" It was almost as if I had caught the Holy Ghost. When I finally caught wind of myself, I noticed all the Preachers and Deacons in the pulpit had cover up their faces, some use napkins, or the announcements that the Church hand out every Sunday to cover their faces; while, others turned their backs. Some even turned away their heads so no one could see them, they were all crying laughing and tried to hide it; including, my Pastor was crying laughing.

In the meantime, when I turned and looked over at my three sons, the two youngest ones were ducking, hiding and laughing with their mouths wide open so no one could see their faces; they both were embarrassed. My oldest son, Wardell, was so angry that my mother-in-law, his grandmother, who was on the nurses' board, rushed over to him to try to calm him down. He got out of his seat and stormed out of the sanctuary. My mother-in-law, his grandmother, and other church members got up from their seats, running after him as well, to try to calm him down.

Afterall, the real God, the All-Powerful, Almighty God took his fake god (the Green Terror fishes) life; instead of him. He should have been praising God with me, he should have been thankful and grateful that God answered my prayer and spared his life. After church let out, some of the Ministers in the church walked up to me and said, "Girl, we love your Testimony about the fishes; that was too funny! You know you don't be playing with your sons," one of the Ministers said while still laughing.

My mother-in-law was so mad with me, as soon as I got home, my house phone rang. It was my mother; my mother-in-law had called her and told her and my husband about how bad I embarrassed my oldest son, Wardell, in church, and, how he stormed out of the church in a rage. My mother was so mad with me, she cursed me out; called me everything but a child of God. She told me that s**t wasn't right what I did, embarrassing her grandson like that.

Wardell Jr., is my first born and is everyone's favorite child; he has a bubbly and silly personality, very mouthy and doesn't like for me to tell him what to do. My husband came home from work and said, "What did you tell the people at the church today? Did you think that I wasn't going to find out?"

"Whatever! I am grown, I can say whatever I want. Maybe, you should try coming to church sometimes, then you will know what I said," I said.

Out of spite, when I came home from work the next day, my son brought some more fishes; more dangerous than the Green Terrors, he brought Piranha fishes. He never asked my permission to buy the fishes, he used his own money from working summer jobs and that didn't sit well with me; at all. I remembered what God had said to me about taking his life and how I had to beg and plead with God to please not take his life. And, the promise I made to God, that it wouldn't happen again.

So, as days went by, my son, Wardell, was back to putting those fishes first before everything; every time, I would tell him to clean his bedroom up, he would say, "Okay, mom. But first, I have to feed my fishes or clean out the fish tank." Which, by the way, had the entire house smelling from being dirty. So, I had enough. The next day before taking my sons to school, I thought about what God had told me about taking my son, Wardell's life, because he had made those fishes his god, again. God said in His First Commandment that, "He is a jealous God, have no other gods before Him." I told my three sons to get in the car, while they were in the car, I went back in the house and poured bleach down in the fish tank then left to take my three sons to school.

After school let out for the day and the boys had made it home, my son, Wardell, called me on my work phone crying, hysterical; I could barely make out what he was saying but I already knew that it had something to do with his fishes. "Mom, my fishes are dead, but I was able to save one of them," he said.

"I am so sorry honey to hear about your fishes, I will see you when I get home," I said as I hung up the phone. When I got home my two youngest sons ran outside to meet me in the driveway and said, "Mom, that dude fishes were dead when we got home. Man' ma, we felt so sorry for him. Man, you should have been home to see that dude, he just sat on his bed and was crying really hard."

"Those fishes didn't die, I killed them. I poured bleach down in the fish tank," I said. They froze dead in their tracks and were in shock, they looked at me in disbelief. They put their heads down, looking pitiful. I told them what God said to me about taking their brother's life because he kept leaving God's house (Church) to go and find his god, the Green Terrors, some feeder fish; so, I killed them so God can spare his life; they were so hurt. Years later, or should I say, even to this day, whenever my son, Wardell, talks about him coming home from school and found his fishes dead and how he was so hurt, my two youngest sons, cut their eyes over at me and just look down towards the floor. He still doesn't know that I killed his fake god (those Piranha fishes); unless, he reads this book.

# "THE EIGHTH COMMANDMENT."

### *THOU SHALL NOT STEAL – EXODUS 20 (KJV)*

One day, my sister, my middle son, and his then girlfriend went out to eat at a local restaurant called; Little Daddy's in Taylor, Michigan. When we walked through the door, there were no one standing at the counter to seat us; as we stood there waiting to be seated, we noticed a sign that said, "Please wait to be seated." The restaurant was empty, so why the sign? As we were waiting for someone to come and seat us, there was a candy jar filled with peppermints, by the register that said, "FREE – Please take one."

My sister, my middle son and his girlfriend at that time, grabbed one peppermint and I decided to grab a hand full. My sister said to me, "The sign said, 'take one.'

"I did take one," I said.

"No, you didn't. You took more than one," said my sister.

"I took one hand full," I said.

"That's called, stealing," my sister said.

"How is that stealing when the note on the jar said, 'FREE,' I said.

"It said, 'take one.' You took more than one and that's stealing," said my sister.

As we stood there going back and forth about me taking a hand full of peppermints, a waiter finally came and seated us at a table by the fireplace, it was cold that day; so, we had requested to sit by the lit-up fireplace to stay warm. After, the waiter took our orders, my sister and I decided to continue our conversation; my middle son and his girlfriend never said anything but just listen to us; as we were debating back and forth about the peppermints.

"It's the same thing at work, I order supplies for everyone on my floor. I bring some supplies home like pencils, highlighters, white-ones, just small things," I said.

"That's called stealing," everyone said.

"No, it's not. The company is not going to mind, they are a billion-dollar company; everybody takes supplies home, all the time," I said.

My sister stopped debating with me and went in her purse and pulled out a handful of different kind of peppermints, the big soft ones that melts in your mouth. "I have some peppermints with Bible Scriptures written on them, do anybody want one?" She asked.

Everybody said, "Yes." She handed each of us one and said, "Read your scriptures out loud, I want to know what everybody says."

While everyone read their scriptures out loud, they were all laughing and said that the writing was so small that they could barely read it. I opened mine up and immediately froze in my chair, I couldn't move; let alone, talk. After everyone finished reading their scriptures, they turned to me and said, "What does yours say?"

"Read it out loud," said my sister.

I couldn't move nor could I say anything, I just sat there looking down at my scripture; so, my sister took my scripture out of my hand, looked at it. Her mouth felled wide open and she showed it to my middle son and his girlfriend, they all read it and immediately jumped up from the table and ran and sat at another table; leaving me to sit at the table, all by myself. The waiter came back and said, "Oh, you guys decided to move to a different table."

They all said at the same time, "We moved. Let her stay over there at the table all by herself; We're not trying to get struck by lightning."

My sister said to me with a smirk on her face, "You just got checked by God. You kept insisting that you weren't stealing, all of ours had small writing on them; whereas, we could barely read them. But yours, was in all caps, big and bold letters that said, '**THOU SHALL NOT STEAL**.' So, you can stay right over there and eat all by yourself."

As soon as I got home, I gathered up all the supplies or anything that I had taken from my job, put them in a bag and returned them to my job the very next day. Weeks later, my job has sent out a memo to every employee that worked for the company, asking everyone that had taken any supplies home; especially, their pencils, to please return all of them; indicating, that they spend millions of dollars every year on just supplies alone and for now on whenever ordering supplies, even if it's just one pencil, and it only cost twenty five cents, it had to be approved only by upper management, before placing an order; because, too many employees were taking supplies home in August, as school was getting ready to start back up, for their children's back to school supplies. I am glad that I had returned everything that I had taken from my job way before they sent that memo out, and I never took anything else from my job.

# "TESTED, WHILE ALREADY IN THE FIRE."

*"But he knows where I am going. And when he tests me, I will come out as pure gold." - Job 23:10 (KJV)*

One day while lying in bed, thinking and crying all night long. I decided that I was sick and tired of being sick and tired, I was alone and lonely; I had no one that I could trust, let alone talk too. I was thinking of how I survived death twice, the first time while I was only 19 years old, living with my play family and having a cyst on my ovaries, and having to have surgery to have it removed. I never said anything to anyone about me having to go in the hospital to have surgery; whereas, the doctor had to go in through my belly button to remove it. As I was laying on the table, I could hear everything that the doctor and nurse were talking about; I heard conversations all around me, even though, I couldn't wake up.

All of a sudden, I heard the Nurse yelling and saying, "We're losing her! We're losing her!" The next thing I knew, they were resuscitating me twice, before I finally came back. And the second time, I escaped death was when I died in my sleep when my sons were one, three and five years old; at the age of 25.

I had divorced my husband of almost 16 years and he made sure that he was going to make my life a living hell just like he had promised; but little did he know, we were going to make each other's life a living hell. It was just me and my sons, my whole life was just a hot mess. I was contemplating taking my own life, twice; to commit suicide. I had hit rock bottom and didn't want to do this thing called life, anymore.

As, I was thinking back as far as I possibly could, my mother had two different boyfriends that from the ages of seven to age ten that would mess with my body, I couldn't tell my mother because the one that was in the Air Force, would pop in every now and then; he stayed with us and he was also a pedophile. He helped us move from Florida to Michigan because my baby-sister was born with a hole in her heart and she needed open heart surgery. They had no Children's Hospital back then in the 60's to do open heart surgery on new born babies; so, we had to move to Michigan, where she spent the first three years of her life in the hospital.

Anyway, this pedophile would always call me into the kitchen, pretending to act like he wanted to show me how to cook. My other sisters were in the living room watching TV while, my mother was at work. She worked afternoons from three p.m. to eleven p.m. at night. School lets out at three p.m. every day; so, she was never home when we got out of school. He was home when we got out of school and had plenty of time to do whatever he wanted to do to me.

He would call me into the kitchen, while my sisters and I was watching a day time soap opera, 'Dark Shadow.' I remember him sitting in the kitchen, in a chair, putting me on his lap and would start touching me inappropriately; fondling my body with his hands, touching my nipples and my private part and tried kissing me while breathing heavily on me; telling me how pretty I was. I wanted to cry, but couldn't because I didn't like this man or his hands touching me; I hated him. He was breathing so heavy on me, as he was touching me.

This one particular day, he took his thing out and was moving it around on my private area, he was about to try to insert it in my private area; when all of a sudden, he heard footsteps walking toward the kitchen, he quickly threw me off of him; fixed himself and pretended like he was trying to explain to me about how to cook. When my sister had left out of the kitchen, he told me to not tell my mother. And, if I tell her, he was going to whip me and that she was not going to believe me and whip me as well; I believed him, and was scared because I didn't want a whipping.

My sister never said anything to me; so, I don't know if she had seen what the pedophile tried to do to me. He did this repeatedly for three years, from seven years old to the age of ten. I had started my period at seven years old. I remember waking up one morning and went to use the bathroom and saw some red stuff in my panties, I ran to my mother and said, "Mom, look! There's ketchup up in my panties."

My mom took me to the doctor, who gave me a shot to stop my period. At age eight, my period came back on, my mom took me back to the doctor again; he gave me another shot to stop my period. At age nine, my period came back on, again. My mom took me back to the doctor again, this time the doctor said, "Her body is just maturing for her age, we can't keep giving her shots to stop her period, we just have to let nature take her course."

Finally, at the age of ten, the pedophile left and I never saw him again; I was so relieved and happy. Then, the second boyfriend came alone, he would see me outside playing, called me over to his car and told me to get in and that he was going to take me to get some ice cream; that I never got. As I got in the car, he immediately started touching me inappropriately; and, the cycle would repeat itself; including telling me how pretty I was. I remember crying at night while lying in bed, "God, I don't want to be pretty no more. Please, make me ugly," I cried.

Now, at 17 years old, right after coming home from school and work, my mother had put me out of her house with only the clothes on my back. I didn't know why and she never told me why. I just remember coming home from work, while in High School, 12th grade, and had a co-op job; working part-time, after school.

After I left work this one particular day, as soon as I walked through the door, my mother had come home from playing cards across the street. She walked up to me and started screaming, yelling and cursing at me, "Get out! Get the hell out of my god damn house!" I was in shock! I didn't know what to do or say; I didn't have a clue as to what was going on.

"Don't take nothing with you, because I brought all of your clothes, don't use my god damn telephone to call no one, because I pay the mother f*ck*ng phone bill. I disown you; when you see me walking down the street, turn your f*ck*ng head; I hate you. Your daddy was nothing, and you ain't never going to be nothing. I wish, I never had you; I wish you were never born, you ain't nothing but a hoe," she said.

I stood there, feeling and looking numb and in shocked at the same time; I had never disrespected my mother, I never talked back to her; especially, if I wanted to live because my mother didn't play with us. She would beat us with an extension cord until she saw blood oozing out of our skin. She put fear in us. So, when she told me that I was nothing but a hoe, this was the first time I ever said anything back to her; I had to stand up for myself because I was a virgin, never did anything with anyone; never ever kissed a boy in my life.

"I didn't know a hoe can be a virgin," I said.

"Get out! Get the hell out of my house and don't come back!" she said as she turned to my sisters and told them that I was nothing but a hoe and not to let me back in her house. I didn't know what to do, or where I was going to go. I had no money and no way of calling anyone; I really thought that she was playing but when I looked in her face and saw the hate in her eyes and heard the rage in her voice, I knew she wasn't playing.

As I walked out of her house and started walking down the street; crying and confused, I was scared; because it will be getting dark soon. I saw this big church, and no one was in the church; so, I decided to sleep on the steps of the church and was hoping that no one saw me. I was rethinking in my mind, how one day I had come home early from work and I overheard my mother and all of my sisters talking bad about me; they never knew that I had come home and heard them.

As I stood at the bottom of the steps, listening to everything they had said about me, I can't lie, I was hurt. I slowly and quietly turned around and walked back out the door. I walked the streets hurting on the inside for about an hour or two and then went back home as if I had just got off of work and just got home. As, I walked in the door, this time making sure that they heard me coming through the door; as soon as they heard me, everyone immediately got quiet.

I just didn't understand what was it that I did wrong and why my family hated me so bad. I had no money and no food, so I went through garbage cans, in hope to find something to eat. Every day, I would walk to find me a different spot to sleep and whenever I would see a loose dog, I got scared, started crying and praying that he wouldn't try to bite me; this was my life for a while. I remember people walking past me and holding their nose because I was beginning to smell really bad, and how embarrassed I was.

One day, I walked to school early from sleeping on the steps of a different church all night long, I snuck in the school building so I could wash up in the girl's bathroom before anyone got there. After getting paid from my job, I was able to catch the bus to school and work. At school, I had this one best friend; her name was Trina.

I met her in the ninth grade, we remained best friends throughout our entire high school years. While in class talking one day, I just decided to tell her that I was homeless, and that my mother had put me out of the house. After school, her and I walked to her house; her mother worked the afternoon shift, so when her mother got off of work late that night; after eleven p.m., she told her mother that I was homeless and that my mother had put me out of the house; she asked her mother if I could stay with them; her mother said, "Yes, you can stay here with us as long as you like, I will never put you out."

One day after coming home from work, my play mother, my play auntie, and my best friend told me that while I was at work, my mother and my sisters had come over to their house and told them to put me out of their house.

"The nerve of that lady coming over here to my house, trying to tell me what to do, in my house; telling me, to put you out of my house. I told her, "This is my house. I am not going to put you out, and that you are a sweet girl; you never gave me any problems and I didn't appreciate her coming over here, trying to tell me what to do in my house. Sine, we were getting ready to jump on your mother; before, we put her out," said my play mother.

"How did she know where I lived at?" I asked.

"We thought you told her," She said.

"No, I haven't spoken to her nor have I seen her since she put me out," I said.

The next day, my play sister and I went over to my mother's house, this was my first time in a while since I had gone over to my mother's house since she put me out with only the clothes on my back. As, I knocked on the door, my oldest sister came to the door and said, "I can't let you in. Mama said that you ain't nothing but a hoe and not to let you in," as she closed the door in my face.

After going back over to the house two more times wanting to get me some clothes; the third time, my oldest sister said to me again, "I can't let you in. Mama said that you ain't nothing but a hoe and not to let you in."

"Open the door and let me in so I can get some of my clothes," I said.

"Nope! You ain't nothing but a hoe," she said as she tried to hurried up and close the door in my face. The next thing I knew, I forced my way into the house. And, as she tried to run up the stairs, I grabbed a hold of her and tried to seriously hurt her. I kicked her butt; she got a beat down that day. My play sister and I went back home and she told everybody in the house what had happened when I tried to go home and get me some clothes to wear, and how my sister kept calling me a hoe.

Besides, she was the one that I had introduced to a man walking down the street, holding his ears and singing; I just happen to be sitting on the porch when he saw me and said, "Hey, do you want to be my girlfriend?"

"No! I already have a boyfriend but I'll introduce you to my sister," I said.

"Okay, where is she?" He asked.

"She'll be home in a minute from school," I said. He waited on the porch with me until she came home. I introduce them and three months later, my sister was pregnant with my niece. I was still a virgin, even, after my niece turned three years old; so, you do the math.

The next day, after I came home from work, my play mother told me that this man came over to the house looking for me and had left his phone number for me to call him, it was my neighbor from across the street that my mother played cards with. I was 17 years old, in the twelfth grade.  And, he was 25 years old, and worked at Ford Motor Company; He came over to the house to talk to me.  I didn't know how he knew where I was living at until he told me that my mother had told him where I was; and, he came over to talk to me. "Do you know why your mother put you out?" He asked.

"No," I said.

"We were playing cards and your mom liked me and I told her that I liked you. And, the next thing I knew, I didn't see you anymore across the street," he said.

I told him what had happened, he apologized and said that it was his fault.  Now, this is a neighbor that I never had a conversation with; all I know is that, whenever I came home from school and work, he was sitting on his porch looking at me, smiling and waving his hand saying hello to me.  I never had a face-to-face conversation with this man and

I never knew he liked me; besides, he had a girlfriend, I would see her over there every now and then and thought nothing of it; my mind was on finishing high school. He started picking me up from work so I didn't have to catch the bus or had to depend on anyone to pick me up.

I had finished high school and not one of my family members; including my sisters, never came to my graduation.  I kept looking out in the audience, hoping that I would see someone from my family there to support me; no, not a one.

After picking me up from work, he came over to the house and we would ride out to Belle Isle Park. This one particular day, after leaving the Park, he stopped at a party store and brought two Cooler drinks. He had pulled up at a Motel, once inside, I went to use the bathroom and when I came out of the bathroom, he handed me my drink; which was already opened.  I drank it and all I remembered after that was being at home; I couldn't remember anything before that.

One day, I was at work and had started bleeding really heavy; one of my co-workers had taken me to the hospital because I was in a lot of pain. Once at the hospital, the doctor told me that I was pregnant and had suffered a miscarriage, and they had to do a D & C (Dilation and Curettage: a brief surgical procedure in which the cervix is dilated and a special instrument is used to scrape the uterine lining.)

Now, I am thinking to myself, how was I pregnant? Considering, I never had sex; I considered myself to still be a virgin.  So, after the miscarriage, I stopped seeing the older guy. Because, obviously, after we left the park and he went to the party store and brought two coolers and when we went inside the Motel, I went to use the bathroom. While, I was in the bathroom, he had to have slipped something in my drink; it wasn't open before I went to use the bathroom, but it was opened when I came out and he handed it to me.

So, after I stopped seeing him and after living with my play family for about two years, I moved out. I was thinking that it was time for me to leave; although, my play mother never told me to get out nor asked me how long do I plan on staying with them, I made up in my mind that I had to leave before she eventually put me out; I didn't want to take the chance of her putting me out; even though, I knew she didn't mind me staying there forever.

Her and my best friend didn't want me to leave. I had the best two years of my life living with them, and, she treated me as if she had giving birth to me; like I was her biological daughter. She never made a difference between me or her daughter, we were both treated equally; with lots of love and protection. For Christmas, she brought us both the same thing; she brought us both lots of Christmas gifts. I had never experienced so much love and happiness before in my life. She was such a true and beautiful churchgoing Christian woman that had so much love in her. Words can't explain, how thankful, grateful, and appreciative I was to have her as my mom. I love you, mama, Lucille Gaston, my play Auntie Ida Gaston, who was the coolest aunt ever; we had so much fun (may her soul rest in peace in heaven, I love you always and miss you dearly, Auntie), and my sweet and crazy sister from another mother, Trina Gaston; and the male crew, Uncle Sydney, Uncle Curtis, Dee, Boo, and Tony. I don't know how we did it, but we made it work in that little small two-bedroom house; we never argued, or fight, we never had any disagreements; it was just pure love and fun; every day. We lived the best of life, no one never made a difference between me or any one of us; if you bothered one of us, you had the entire house that you had to go through. The house probably was sane until I moved in and me and my crazy sister, Trina, was like females; Bonnie and Clyde.

Shortly after I moved out of her house, I lived with my boyfriend who later became my husband. I started thinking about my husband, again, how he was abusive to me while he was only my boyfriend, and at the same time, knowing that I should have never married him or had any children with him- but that's what happens when you don't use protection. I thought that I couldn't get pregnant because for two years being intimate with him and not taking anything; nothing happened. So, for certain, I thought I was infertile and couldn't get pregnant; I played with fire, until I got burned!

After, I moved in with my boyfriend, I became pregnant with my first child. I had gone into labor, I had never seen or heard from my mother in two years. So, while I was in labor, in walks my mother; in my hospital room, I was truly shocked to see her. I didn't even know that she knew I was pregnant, let alone in labor. I was the only one in the labor room when my mother walked in, came over to me and said, "they told me that you were in labor, getting ready to have a baby. I didn't believe it and I just had to come and see for myself. You caused me so much pain when I was in labor with you, that I almost died. I wish that you would die on that table having your baby."

"Nurse! Nurse! Get her out of my room, now! I don't want her in here," I said as the Nurse came running in my room.

Once the nurse put my mother out of my room, I couldn't stop crying and thinking about how my mother hated me so bad; she had the nerve to come here, to the hospital, while I am in labor, only to wish death on me. Six weeks after, I had my son, my mother surprisingly, called me out of the blue and said, "I don't care if I never see you again, just let me see my grandson." I allowed her to come over to the house to see him, even though, I don't know how she got my phone number or my address; perhaps she got it from my baby daddy.

Every time, I got pregnant, I prayed, rubbed my stomach with holy oil (olive oil) that my Pastor had prayed over and said, "God, please let it be a boy." I didn't want to have a daughter because I was afraid of repeating the generational cycle, I didn't want to bring a daughter into this world; only to mistreat her. I didn't know if I could love a daughter only because of how my mother treated me, and I never denied my mother the right from seeing any of my sons. I loved her, regardless of how she felt about me. I never had any bad feelings towards her; in spite, of how she treated me. I always respected her and treated her with love and kindness until I finally won her over. She eventually started accepting me and allowed me to come over to the house; after, I had my sons.

After my boyfriend and I got married, every time I got pregnant, he would cheat, and the mental and physical abuse would follow. So, I got my tubes tied to keep from having any more children by this man. Five years after being married to this man, I guess his conscious was eating away at him. He came and confessed to me that when I was staying with my play mother and when someone had stolen my car from in front of the house; he said that my mother paid him to steal my car.

I wished that I had known this before I married him, I would have never married this man. Even after I divorced him, he threatened me and claimed that he hired someone to kill me and that the police wouldn't be able to come after him because he will be in Florida; out of town. And, that he had keys to my van and he was working on getting keys to my car and when I come home from work, that my house was going to be burned down.

"Well, if you hired someone to kill me, then you'd better make sure they kill me because if they don't, then I am coming after you; and, I will kill you. And, you better make sure that you put your mama up in a hotel; because, that blue barn that she's living in, I am going to burn it down. So, if my sons and I are not going to have a roof over our heads, your mama is not going to have a roof over her head," I said.

I went down to the police station to put a PPO (Personal Protection Order) against him, he ignored the PPO and kept getting into my house trying to force himself on me, calling me and threatening me all day on my cell phone, my home phone and my work phone. The PPO that I placed against him said for him not to come on my property and not to call me on my cell, home or work phone. I took him to court twice and I won; he took me to court twice and I still won. So, he decided to call me after leaving court and said, "I can't win against you, I will never bother you again nor will I ever put my hands on you, again."

"You may be stronger than me physically, but I am stronger than you spiritually; so, therefore, you can't win against me," I said.

The next thing I knew, he took my brand-new van from church while the boys were at choir rehearsal, him and his younger brother because someone saw them sitting in a car behind my van, waited for everyone to go inside the church and stole my van from the church; they had poured gasoline all over it and set it on fire. Chrysler said that they wanted $1,000 a week and that they were going to start garnishing me; I tried to compromise with them, offering them $500 a month; they refused and said, "$1,000 a week." They were truly playing hard ball with me and not bulging.

I told them that I didn't make that kind of money, and I will lose my house and couldn't afford to pay that. They basically told me in so many words, that wasn't their problem; they wanted their money. I leased a brand-new van from them and now I don't have the vehicle anymore and they want $1,000 every week or they will garnish me; I had to file bankruptcy. The bankruptcy attorney had me file a Chapter Seven, but when I went to court, the judge asked me if I wanted to keep my house, "Yes," I said. The Judge then told me that I filed the wrong

Chapter, that I should have filed a Chapter 13 if I wanted to keep my house. My attorney had the audacity to tell me that he doesn't do Chapter 13 bankruptcies and that I would have to find me a Chapter 13 bankruptcy Attorney, pay him and start all over; again. Boy, was I mad; now I have two Bankruptcies on my credit file; a seven and a thirteen?

With everything happening in my life, I had come to the conclusion that I was going to just end it all; I did not want to live anymore.  I laid in bed contemplating how I wanted to end my life, 'I am going to take this entire bottle of medication; but first, I am going to kiss every one of my sons, that would be my final 'goodbye' kiss; so, when they wake up, they would already find me dead.  But, after, I kissed my son's, I was going to go down on my knees first and thanked God for everything that He has ever done for me,' I said.

I put the bottle of medication right on my bed, I went into each one of my son's bedroom quietly, so I wouldn't wake them. I kissed them all while they were sleeping and whispered to them softly, "I love you." I went back into my bedroom, grabbed the bottle of medication, got down on my knees and started thanking God for everything that He has ever done for me. This is where the devil messed up, he should have killed me before I went down on my knees and prayed to God and thanked Him.

*"I will never leave you nor forsake you, I am with you always even until the end of the world,"* said God.

"God! You saw what I went through. You were there when my husband tried to kill me, throwing me on the floor while sitting on top of me, beating and choking me until I passed out. Putting his hands on me; punching me, throwing me up against the wall, knocking my head against the wall, bruised my ribs; and, me having to walk around with dark sun glasses on; so, no one can see my black eyes.

Him cheating on me, throughout, the entire marriage.

"God, you were there when my mother boyfriends were messing with my body. You were there when my mother put me out, you were right there, God!  And, you allowed me to go through it, you allowed all of that to happen to me, and you never said a word. Why God? Why me?" I asked, while sobbing at the same time.

*"Why not you!" said God, very firm.*

*"My child, you must first be tested and tried through the fire in order to be made whole, you are going to go through some of everything," said God.*

The next thing I knew, it was morning. I had fallen asleep, waking up, still on my knees from talking to God and God must have erased that day from my memory because two months later, I am just now trying to remember what happened to the bottle of medication that I was going to take. God had put me to sleep and removed the bottle of medication or I may have thrown the entire bottle of medication out. I can't remember for the life of me, what happened to that bottle of medication.

After contemplating suicide, in which, I failed at because God intervened and assured me that He was never going to leave me nor forsake me and that He was going to be with me even until the end of the world. "I apologize to you Father God; please forgive me for everything that I did wrong," I said.

God deals with our hearts. You can't go to God and ask for forgiveness, if you have not forgiven someone of the wrong that they did to you; nor, can you ask for forgiveness, if you are not willing to forgive. Before you consider going to God in prayer to ask for forgiveness, you must first forgive and then, ask to be forgiven. You can fool man but you can't fool God. God knows if we are sincere or not; He knows if we have true repentance in our hearts or not.

God is going to hold every one of us accountable for our own actions, whatever part we played in doing right or doing wrong; so, I highly recommend that you choose to do right. You have to want to renew your mind of doing right. Romans 12:2 (NIV), says, *"Do not conform to the pattern of this world, but be transformed by the renewing of your mind. Then you will be able to test and approve what God's will is – his good, pleasing and perfect will."*

Regardless of who did wrong first; He will surely deal with us one on one. You won't be able to point the blame or finger on anyone, we will have to answer to God for what we did or didn't do. Mama or daddy will not be able to save you, you have to save yourself; it will be, every man for themselves. Yes, I said daddy, dad, or pops or whatever you choose to call your dad because the scripture says in Matthew 23:9 (NLV),

*"And do not call anyone on earth 'father,' for you have one Father, and he is in heaven."*

One day, I went to God in prayer and asked Him to forgive me, "Lord, please forgive me for all of my sins. Lord, I have not always been a good wife, a good mother, a good daughter, a good sister nor a good friend. Father God, I have done more wrong than right but I am asking for forgiveness.  Please, Lord, please forgive me," I asked.

*"In order for me to forgive you, you must first forgive your husband,"* *said God.*

"God, what do you mean I have to first forgive my husband?  You were right there, you saw everything. You saw what that man did to me. He did wrong to me; even, tried to kill me! And, I have to forgive him?" I questioned God angrily.

While thinking in my mind, 'I divorced him, so why would God call this man my husband. He cheated on me and I returned the favor and cheated on him; besides, God, himself said, "Grounds for divorce is committing adultery only. We both committed adultery, and he said that you have to physically catch him in the act; in which, I did.  He had this girl in my house, in my bedroom and I took my hand and tried to snatch the balls off of him. That's when he jumped up out of the bed and jumped on me in front of her; putting my head in the wall.  Now, don't get me wrong, I may not could have beaten him physically, but he felt a piece of me; I fought him back,' as I was thinking about all of this while listening to God.

Now, when God didn't say anything back to me, I became afraid. I said to myself, "Maxine, shut your mouth!  Who do you think you are, arguing with God?  God can take your last breath away from you, you are really stupid! And, God knows that you are really stupid; as well."

Every day for nine months, I would pick up the phone to call my ex-husband and try to apologize to him but I couldn't do it.  I would lay down in bed and said his name, I immediately got mad. Just to say or hear his name would make me mad and that's how I knew that I had not forgiven him.  I became worried because months had gone by and I still had not forgiven this man but I wanted God to forgive me.

"God, I can't do it.  I can't forgive my ex-husband, and if I say that I forgive him, you can strike me down dead for lying to you. You know my heart; you know how bad I hate this man. I would spit on the ground wherever he would walk just to make sure I didn't walk the same path. Lord, you are going to have to show me how to forgive this man; if you want me to forgive him. I hate him more than I hate the devil and you know this. I can't do it, Lord! I can't do it, Lord! Please, show me and help me to love and forgive this man because I can't do it," I said while crying and screaming at God.

The next day, I heard a small voice say, *"Wardell,"* and I didn't get mad, for the first time in ten months. That's when I knew that I no longer hated him, that's when I knew that I had forgiven him. So, I picked up the phone and called him. "Yes, Max," he answered the phone as if he was waiting and expecting me to call him. "Wardell, I am calling you to ask you to forgive me for everything that I have done wrong to you," I said.

"Max," he said as he begins to sobbed on the phone. "I forgive you; I hope you forgive me as well. Max, you were a good wife, you didn't do anything wrong; I listened to other people and ruined my marriage. I know that you are not going to believe me and I know that I have never told you this in the 15 years while we were married, that I love you. I really do love you," he said while still sobbing as he was talking to me.

"You are right, I don't believe you. I only called you because God told me that I had to forgive you, before He can forgive me. I love you too but only as a brother-in-Christ and nothing more, I am not calling trying to get back with you," I said.

"That's fine, Max. But I do love you," he said.

After that one phone call, he would call me every year to wish me a happy birthday and offered to take me out to eat for my birthday; that's funny, when we were married for almost 16 years, he never remembered my birthday and would always work double shifts to keep from spending time with me on my birthday. And, whenever I asked him to let's go out to dinner to eat, he would go in the kitchen and started cooking. And, whenever I asked him to go to the movies, he would put a DVD on the TV, to watch. Whenever, I would ask him to let's take the boys out and get ice cream, he would say, "I don't eat ice cream."

Now, I was a tattle-tail throughout my entire marriage. Whenever he would do me wrong, I went in my bedroom, got down on my knees and talked to God. I told Him everything what this man was doing wrong to me. I would say, "Lord, this man that I married and I already know that you know what is going on in my marriage but, because you said Father God, that you already know what we have need of, before we even ask of you and, because, you also said Father God that, 'we have not, because we ask not.' So, I am asking you Father God to bless me with this or with that. Now, I know heavenly Father, that no man works overtime for two months straight, and not take one day off. Father God, if he's out there doing anything that he's not supposed to be doing, please show me Father God. Lead me straight to him and show me."

As soon as I got off of my knees from praying and talking to God, my oldest son came in my bedroom and said, "Mom, can we go and get some Taco Bell?"

"Sure. Taco Bell is right across the street from Dairy Queen, I will take you guys to get Taco Bell and I will get some Dairy Queen," I said. As we went to Taco Bell first and got our orders, the boys and I went across the street and got Dairy Queen. After, we had gotten our Dairy Queen and I was about to pull off to go home, I just so happened to turn my head and saw my husband; sitting in his car, at Dairy Queen.

"I don't believe this," I said.

"What mom? What don't you believe?" asked my sons.

"Your dad! I don't believe your dad is sitting in his car with a girl and eating ice cream with her, when I had just asked him yesterday to let's go and get some ice cream and he told me that he don't eat ice cream; and, he had just called me from his job and told me that he was working overtime and fifteen minutes later, here he is sitting in his car, eating ice cream," I said.

God led me straight to Him, just like I had prayed and asked. I parked the car, got out, and as I was approaching his car, I saw him looking at me through his mirror. "I thought you told me that you don't eat ice cream," I said while bending over looking in the car. "By the way, I am his wife," I said.

"I know. I know who you are, I am not trying to start any trouble," she said nervously.

"You can have him because he's not coming back home to me, I don't want him," I said as I reached in the car and took his ice cream and smashed it in his face.  As, I proceeded to walk away, he jumped out of his car, to do what? To hit me? I don't think so; not this time, this sister was ready for anything that day.

"Do it! I dare you to hit me! Go ahead and hit me and we will both tear this parking lot up; with the boys and everybody watching," I said.  He never said not one word to me; especially, after he realized that the boys were in the car watching the both of us. While he was wiping the ice cream off of his face, I walked back to my car and pulled off; it was a long and silent ride all the way back home.

When the boys and I got back home, my oldest son was literally shaking and very upset said to me, "Mom, are you going to put that dude out?"

"I sure am," I said as my sons and I started gathering up all of his stuff. "His mama can wash his filthy, nasty, stinky, dirty clothes," I said as I was gathering up all of his stuff; mixing clean clothes with the dirty clothes; along with the dry clean, and placed them all in one big super large garbage bag. The boys and I then drove over to his mama's house, threw everything of his out of the car and into the middle of the driveway, rang the doorbell and my sons and I jumped into the car and pulled off.  Once in the car and back at home, I called a locksmith to come over and changed the locks.  After the locks were changed, I called my husband and said, "Don't worry about coming back home, I threw all of your stuff out. They're in your mama's driveway and I got the locks changed so you can't get back in," I said.

"I am coming back home and I am getting back in my house," he said.  I guess after seeing all of his belongings over at his mama's house, in the driveway, he never came back over.  His mama had called me the next day and said, "I don't know what's wrong with these men, they won't act right and expect someone to wash their clothes."

The day after that, my mother-in-law came over to my house and said, "Maxine, I came over to talk to you."

"You need to be talking to your son and not me; especially, if you care about his life," I said.

*"From the same mouth come blessing and cursing. My brothers, these things ought not to be so." James 3:10 (ESV)*

*"To speak evil of no one, to avoid quarreling, to be gentle, and to show perfect courtesy toward all people." Titus 3:2 (ESV)*

*"A time to tear, and a time to sew; a time to keep silence, and a time to speak." Ecclesiastes 3:7 (ESV)*

*"Set a guard, O Lord, over my mouth; keep watch over the door of my lips!" Psalm 141:3 (ESV)*

*"A soft answer turns away wrath, but a harsh word stirs up anger." Proverbs 15:1 (ESV)*

*"If anyone thinks he is religious and does not bridle his tongue but deceives his heart, this person's religion is worthless." James 1:26 (ESV)*

*"Whoever keeps his mouth and his tongue, keeps himself out of trouble." Proverbs 21:23 (ESV)*

*"Let the words of my mouth and the meditation of my heart be acceptable in your sight, O Lord, my rock and my redeemer." Psalm 19:14 (ESV)*

"Lord, I tell you, you have that Cora mouth; you are just like your mama. The Bible said that the older women are to teach the younger women, you are the woman of the house and it's your job to keep peace in the home. Whenever he gets to cutting up, you just be quiet. Men are always wrong; you just have to let them think that they are right," she said. I listened and took her advice; I valued her opinion. She is my elder, and I respect all of my elders; especially, my mother-in-law, whom I look up to and love dearly.

One day, I took the boys over to see my mother-in-law and my husband were over there as well. My youngest son wanted some potatoes chips that was on the table; it was lots of goodies on the table, so when he went to grab a bag of chips, my husband grabbed and snatched the bag out of his hands.

"Why did you snatch the bag of chips out of his hand?" I asked.

"If you don't like it, I will put my hands on you," said my husband.

"I am not worried about you putting your hands on me," I said.

The next thing I knew, my husband jumped up from the table and tried to hit me and my mother-in-law grabbed him and said, "I didn't raise you like that to put your hands on no woman, you know better than that. You never saw your dad put his hands on me."

"Oh, yes I did," he said.

"When have you ever saw your dad put his hands on me?" She asked.

"I'd seen dad hit you several times," he said.

"Name me one time that you saw your dad put his hands on me," she said.

"When dad came home from work this one day and he wanted to have sex and he told you to go upstairs and you told him that you were tired. That's when he took his hand and slapped you across your face and he told you to get upstairs now. And, after, he slapped you across your face, you went upstairs like a good little wife," he said to his mother.

My sons and I left, the next day, my mother-in-law called me and said, "Maxine, I am so sorry about yesterday, he wasn't raised like that and I didn't know that he had seen his dad hit me; I thought that they were too young to remember that incident."

"So, he watched how his dad treated you, and he's trying to treat me the way his dad treated you. So, this is a learned behavior.

And, my mom used to fight all the time, I found that out when her cousin came into town and she was telling me about my mom and her fighting; beating up everybody, she didn't care who you were; if you walked on two's, male or female, she wasn't afraid of you; she would fight you. So, that's where I got my fighting from, from my mom; I would fight anybody, I didn't care who you were; if you walked on two's, male or female, I wasn't afraid of you; I would fight you; a generational curse.

A learned behavior plus a generational curse equal a disaster," I said.

# "YOU ARE JUST LIKE JONAH."

*"OBEDIENT IS BETTER THAN SACRIFICE."- 1 Samuel 15:22*

One day while singing in the choir at church, God spoke to me and said, *"I do not want you to sing in the choir, I want you to deal with the youth."*

"Lord, I don't want to deal with the youth, they are hard headed," I said.

*"You are hard-headed; you are just like Jonah, I tell you to do one thing and you do the complete opposite,"* God said back to me. (You can read the entire story about Jonah and the whale, Jonah, Chapters 1 – 4 NIV).

Needless to say, I kept singing in the choir and the Lord said to me again, *"I do not want you to sing in the choir, I want you to deal with the youth."*

Singing was a passion of mine; all I wanted to do was sing. I step down from the choir but I did not deal with youth. I would come to church every Sunday and three years later, I thought that God had forgot about when He told me to not sing in the choir, but to deal with the Youth. So, I rejoined the choir and immediately I started to have trouble with my throat; every time I tried to sing a note or anything, it felt like someone had taken a knife and slit my throat; I was in excruciating pain. I made an appointment to see an ETN (ears, throat and nose) doctor; after examining me and sticking tubes down my throat, he couldn't find out what the problem was. I got tired of them sticking tubes down my throat which was painful, and those tubes were starting to make my throat worse, so I stopped going to see them, wasting my time and money.

Whenever, I tried to sneak back into the choir, my throat would start bothering me again. God eventually made my voice where I couldn't sing anymore. I finally decided to be obedient; I got out of the choir permanently and joined the youth staff, being an assistant to the Youth Pastor. Now, I don't know for the life of me why I ran from God, dealing with the Youth became my passion. I enjoyed working with the youth (ages 12-18) so much, they became my babies; I got to know them and loved them so much and the next thing I knew, I was helping assist in teaching Sunday school, Vacation Bible School and speaking at the Youth Scholarship Banquet and speaking at church every third Sunday of the month for the Youth Service Program. I even volunteered to join the after-school tutoring program to help children of all ages that was having trouble with their homework, improving their grades at school, so they can qualify for the church youth scholarships; and I made my sons help volunteer as well. My Pastor gave me keys to the church van so I volunteered to drive all across town picking children up for choir rehearsal and taking them back home; to my surprise, my husband volunteered to help me drive as well; so, the parents wouldn't have to worry about getting their children to the church or how they were going to get back home.

My sons helped volunteer as well; in which, they didn't mind. They just jumped right in, never complained and did whatever the church needed them to do. They sang in the choir and were junior ushers as well, all while going to school, and maintaining good grades. We helped served dinners every third Saturday at church to help feed the hungry. I have to admit, God is awesome and I enjoyed every task and assignment that He threw my way and wished that I had never ran from Him; but was obedient, it was the best thing that God could have had me to do. Even though, I was working full time and would rush home from work just to get to the church, the good thing is, I never got tired; God made my body to do whatever the church needed me to do and do it cheerfully.

Dealing with the Youth became my babies and my passions; even though at first, I was scared to the point where my knees had literally started shaking and I thought they were going to fall off of my body. Actually, I got tricked into volunteering all of those things at church because once I joined the youth staff, I noticed that everyone at church did less. They would purposely come late so that I can take charge, I was so scared and nervous, but I did it because I was enjoying what the Lord told me to do. Some of the members in the church would come up to me and say, "Sister Maxine, Sister Pat is running late and asked us to have you to start the service or program for her."

And, there were times when I overheard some of the church member say, "Have Sister Maxine to speak at the youth scholarship banquet, I want her to do it because she is really good at dealing with the youth; I am going to stand back and let her take charge." That's when I realized that I was being set up, being pushed out of my comfort zone; once, I became obedient to God, He used my sons and I for His glory. That was the best thing that has ever happened to us.

# "NO MAN HAS SEEN GOD AND LIVED."

*"And he said, thou canst not see my face: for there shall no man see me, and live." - Exodus 33:20*

Every night before going to bed, I would pray and talk to God before falling asleep. While talking with him, I noticed that God himself would always come down from heaven and visit me; allowing me to feel His Holy Spirit. His Spirit presence was so strong in my bedroom, I actually knew exactly where His Spirit was at in my bedroom. I would smile and say, "God is in the room, He came down from Heaven to visit me." After feeling His presence, I would fall asleep feeling so loved and protected; knowing that He was in my bedroom, watching over me. His Spirit was so sweet, so loving, so kind, and so gentle; I really can't describe it, it was just that awesome; I just know that I didn't want Him to leave. He always waited for me to fall asleep and when I woke up in the morning, He was gone; I was still hoping that His presence was still in my bedroom. This was His nightly routine; every night, for months. He always came down and visited me before I went to sleep, He never said anything but He made His presence known.

After waking up every morning with God on my mind, reminiscing about last night and feeling God's presence, I couldn't wait to go to bed every night just so I can feel God's presence; again, and again and again. This went on every night for a while, then one night while lying in bed, praying and talking to God as was my nightly routine, I begin to notice that I haven't felt God's presence in a while.

I became very sad and said, "God, I use to feel very close to you, I use to feel your Holy presence every night. I haven't felt your presence in a while, can you please come down and allow me to feel your Holy presence? I miss you, God so much and I love you, I just want to feel your presence," I prayed until I felled asleep.

While my husband and I was sleeping, I felt something touch me. "Hum!" I said as I woke up. Now, the room was completely dark, and we slept with our bedroom door closed so no light can shine through. As I laid there, I saw this big, bright white hand, it pointed to the left of me by the wall; I slept on the side by the wall. I turned my head the way the hand had pointed and saw my youngest son sleeping next to me. He had slipped into our bed in the middle of the night and had no cover on him, he was laying against the wall; shivering. "Okay," I said and the hand left.

Immediately, I sat up; shaking my husband. "Wardell, wake up," I said.

"What Max?" He said.

 "Did you just touch me?" I asked.

"No, Max," he said.

"Something touched me," I said. Then immediately, I remembered my prayer. I had prayed and ask God to let me feel his presence because I haven't felt His Holy presence in a while.

"It was God who touched me, He came down from Heaven and touched me. I know it was Him because He laid his hand so gentle, and so soft on my chest.  He allowed me to see His hand, and He didn't take my life," I said as I was lying in bed thinking about the scripture in Exodus, Chapter 33, verse 20 which said, "No man can see God's face and live." I was so happy because not only did God came down from Heaven, but He touched me.  His hand were so soft and so gentle that I felt His hand print still on my chest when I woke up that day, I wished that I could have grabbed His hand and never let go of it.

# "TITHES AND OFFERINGS."

*8. "Will a man rob God? Yet ye have robbed me. But ye say, wherein have we robbed thee? In tithes and offerings. 9. Ye are cursed with a curse: for ye have robbed me, even this whole nation,"*

## TESTING GOD IN THE TITHES

*10. "Bring all the tithes into the storehouse so there will be enough food in my Temple. If you do, 'says the LORD of Heaven's Armies, 'I will open the windows of heaven for you. I will pour out a blessing so great you won't have enough room to take it in! Try it! Put me to the test!" 11. And I will rebuke the devourer for your sakes, and he shall not destroy the fruits of your ground; neither shall your vine cast her fruit before the time in the field, saith the LORD of hosts."- Malachi 3:10-11 (NLT)*

The Bible speaks about giving ten percent of our income to the church; giving two, four, or six percent is not *tithing*. To tithe is to give 10 percent of your income (before taxes are taken out). Offerings are considered gifts, given in addition to your tithes. The ten percent is 'holy,' and belongs to God; we are given back to God what is already his.

*9. "Honor the Lord with your wealth and the first part of your harvest.*
*10. Then your barns will be full of grain, and your barrels will be overflowing with wine."*
*Proverbs 3:9-10 (ERV)*

*2 Corinthians 9:6-7 (ERV) says about 'The Cheerful Giver'.*
*6. "Remember this: The one who plants few seeds will have a small harvest. But the one who plants a lot will have a big harvest.*
*7. Each one of you should give what you have decided in your heart to give. You should not give if it makes you unhappy or if you feel forced to give. God loves those who are happy to give (a cheerful giver.)"*

One day while lying in bed, I was struggling to make ends meet. I didn't know how I was going to pay my mortgage, take care of my sons; let alone pay my bills. I had stopped paying my taxes just so I can have extra money to pay my bills; and to make matters worse, I got audited by the IRS; they audited me back five years for not paying my taxes in five years; they wanted me to show proofs of my income (W2's) back from five years, as well as other documents and a list of things they wanted by a certain deadline; or else, they were going to garnish my wages, put a lien on my house, take whatever assets I owned and seize all of my money; including, checking, and savings accounts, any stocks or bonds and any IRA's that I might have. I was so mentally drained and overwhelmed by everything that I stopped paying my bills; including, my car payment on a black Ford Taurus, that I loved so much.

One day after coming home from work, I ran in the house to use the bathroom. I was only in the bathroom every bit of two minutes when all of a sudden, I heard a loud screeching noise. I ran to the front door, open it and looked up the street only to see my car being towed away; Ford Motor Company had repossessed my vehicle. As I sat down on the sofa by the front door, I heard a small still voice say, *"Everything is going to be alright, Maxine,"* the voice that people always say they hear. I only hear God speaking to me, very plain and clear.

"Okay," I said.

I immediately felt calm and didn't worry about anything; I didn't worry about the IRS, about how I was going to get to work, about paying my bills, nor how my sons and I were going to make it. Unexpectedly and surprisingly the very next day after coming home from work, my youngest son's girlfriend had let me use her car to go to work, I received three large checks in the mail from the Friend of the Court. During my divorce, my attorney must had set it up whereas I receive child support; that I completely forgot about because I never went down to 'The Friend of The Court' and filed anything. Even though the checks were unexpected, they were right on time and very much needed.

The next day after depositing all three checks in my checking account, I went down to an Auction and bid on three vehicles, won the bids. I may have had one car repossessed, but God blessed me with three large checks, enough to buy me three vehicles paid for in cash. I no longer had to worry about anyone taking my cars from me, and I still had enough money left over in my checking account to make sure that I was able to care for my sons and give them weekly allowances.

My youngest son had an accident in one of my cars and totaled it. So, to teach him a lesson, I made him go and buy a car in his name, so the next time he has an accident in the car, it would be in his name and his car insurance. I ended up using his car that he brought for me to go to work, and whatever else I needed to do, I paid his car note since I was using it for work, kept up all of the maintenance and everything on the car and he never asked for it back; never said anything to me about driving his car.

I had taken a home equity loan out against my house to fix it up after divorcing my husband of almost 16-years of marriage; although, we separated one year before me divorcing him; I was sick and tired of the infidelity, the mental and physical abuse. Him setting my brand-new van on fire that I had just leased from Chrysler with only seven miles on it for my sons to drive themselves to and from school, to ease some of the load off of me. He had my lights and gas shut off in the middle of the winter and had a code put on the account so that I couldn't have them turned back on. I had to send my sons to stay with my mother because it was a very bad and cold winter; lots of snow, until I could figure out how to get them back on.

One day while lying in bed, I heard God's voice. *"Maxine, pay your tithes."* He didn't have to tell me twice; the first thing I did when I got paid was Tithes first, paid myself second (hid money away inside my home for saving and emergency purposes only) and everyone else got whatever was left over, third. After fifteen months of putting myself on a strict diet, budgeting five dollars a day for breakfast, lunch, and dinner from McDonald's one dollar menu, I paid everything except my mortgage. I purposely did not pay my mortgage, now going on fifteen months, allowing my home to go into foreclosure. I was getting nervous and anxious coming home from work every day, worried that my mortgage company had sat all of my stuff out on the street. Finally, I called my Mortgage company and asked them when are they going to sit my things out on the street, the young man on the other end of the phone said, "What is your account number?"

I gave him my account number and he pulled up my account and said, "Ma'am, your account is fifteen months behind in payments, they should have been sat you out. How they overlooked your account is a mystery to me; they normally don't allow anyone to go past three months before they send you an eviction notice.  Do you mind if I put you on hold, I have to discuss your situation over with my manager?" He asked.

"Sure, I don't mind holding," I said.

He came back to the phone and said, "My manager has to review your account; so, we will get back with you tomorrow."

"Ok, thanks," I said.

The next day after I got off of work, the young man from the mortgage company called me back and said, "My manager reviewed your account and said, since you are so far behind on your mortgage, we can't refinance you, and you don't qualify for any of our other home programs; he's willing to make you an offer that you can't refuse.  The good news is this, you can stay in your home, we are not going to put you out.  All you have to do is give us 10 percent of the balance owed on your mortgage and the house is yours free and clear."

"What do you mean give you guys 10 percent of the balance owed on my mortgage and the house is mind free and clear?  How much is 10 percent? And, I want to see that in writing; first," I said.

"Hold on while I calculate everything for you, your Mortgage that you owe is $48,000 plus the taxes and interest comes to $5,500; that's 10 percent on everything, and you have to pay it within thirty days," he said.

I couldn't believe what I was hearing, I thought to myself, 'Look at God, one day he spoke to me while lying in my bed and said, "Maxine, pay your tithes."  And, because I was obedient and paid my tithes for those fifteen months, not cheating him and, I paid Him first before anyone got anything from me. I wrote a check out for my tithes and offering, then I waited for that check to clear so that nothing would interfere with God's money.  Once that check cleared, I paid myself; either matching my tithes and offering or I would save half of what my tithes and offering was; depending on what bills had to be paid, that was what I would put aside in my savings every pay day. So, after calculating everything up, there were only one problem, I had just given my mother $5,000 to get her house of out foreclosure and caught up and paid a lot of her bills. I still had enough money saved up to either pay my son's car off or pay the Mortgage off; but I only had $5,000 and they want me to pay them $5,500; I was $500 dollars short.

I called my sons and explained my situation with the house and the mortgage company and that I had decided to turn down the offer and let the house go and move into an apartment, they said to me, "Mom, don't let the house go." My oldest son said to me, "Mom, my wife and I have decided to loan you the entire $5,500 to pay the house off."

They wired the full amount in my checking account and I wired the money over to the mortgage company. And the mortgage company sent me a 'short sale' noticed in the mail showing that my mortgage was paid in full, zero balance, and my house was mine free and clear just like they said. I paid my oldest son and his wife back for the money they had loaned me. Then I paid my youngest son's car off with my private stashed that I saved up, that was in his name. After I paid his car off, my youngest son came over and handed me the title to the car and said, "Here mom, since you paid the car off and I never paid not one car note, you paid for the car insurance and all of the repairs and everything when it came to dealing with that car, it's your car. I never did anything with the car so you can have the car; besides, I went and brought me a new car yesterday. Since, I wrecked your and you had no other way to get to work, you can have the car; you paid it off."

Look at God! Won't he do it! God is good all of the time and all of the time God is good. He paid my house off, and blessed me to save up enough money to pay my car off. I made arrangement to pay the IRS but paid them off as well. And, I moved up from the five dollars budget menu, to eating regular food or a combo meal at McDonald's. My mother was good for a while, thank you, Jesus! It was hell and it was hard but God saw us through it. One day, I was struggling to make ends meet and because I was obedient and did exactly what God told me to do, God blessed me and reduced my debts from $80,000 to $13,000. Won't God do it! Thank you, Jesus. I love you so much Heavenly Father and I am not ashamed to let the whole world know it. What He has done for me, He will do the same thing for you!

When you pay your tithes, God said in *Malachi 3:10-11;*

*"Bring all the tithes into the storehouse so there will be enough food in my Temple. If you do, 'says the LORD of Heaven's Armies, 'I will open the windows of heaven for you. I will pour out a blessing so great you won't have enough room to take it in!* **Try it! Put me to the test!"**

*"And I will rebuke the devourer for your sakes, and he shall not destroy the fruits of your ground."*

For one year and three months (15 months) God did just that, He said if we bring _all_ of the tithes into the storehouse that He would rebuke the devourer for my sake; for fifteen months, never once the devourer (my mortgage company) called me demanding any money, never once did the devourer threatened to put me out but instead ask me only for the (tithing) 10 percent of the balance owed on the Mortgage and I got to stay in my house, and the house is mine; free and clear.

God wants us to try Him; put Him to the test to see if He won't do what He said He will do. I triple dare you to put God to the test. He will open the windows of Heaven for you and pour you out a blessing so great that you won't have room enough to receive it.

## *TESTIMONY #15:*
# "GOD'S WARNINGS: NOT OBEYING THE VOICE OF GOD."

## EXHIBIT ONE:

## *"DO NOT GO TO CHURCH, DO NOT MOVE YOUR CAR."*

As I was driving home one Wednesday on the Lodge Freeway in Michigan, heading north, my sister called me.

"Hey, Maxine. The church is having a really good service Friday night, do you want to go?" she asked.

"Sure, what time does the service start?" I asked.

"It starts at seven p.m.  But I am leaving early so that I can get me a good parking spot and a good seat inside the church, so I probably will leave the house around 4:30 p.m.  I want to be able to get there by 5:00 p.m. because traffic should be at least slowing down by then," she said.

"Ok, I will meet you over at your house before 4:30 p.m., so I can ride with you," I said.

*"Do not go to church, do not move your car," said a voice from out of nowhere.*

As I look in my rear-view mirror to see where the voice was coming from and to see who was in the back seat, I panicked.  The speed limit was 55 mph, I began to press on the gas pedal and I said to my sister, "Girl, you are not going to believe this?"

"Believe what," she said.

"Something just said, 'Do not go to church, do not move your car," I said.

"Girl, if something just spoke to you and told you not to go to church and not to move your car, then you're not getting in my car," she said.

My mother got on the phone and asked, "What did a voice say to you?"

It said, "*Do not go to church, do not move your car,*" I said.

"You are not getting in your sister car," said my mother.

"That's nothing but the devil that doesn't want me to go to church. I am going to church," I said.

"Girl, you are on your own, you are not getting in my car," my sister said.

"Whatever, I will just drive my own car," I said as I hung up from talking to her.

*"Do not go to church, do not move your car,"* said the voice, again.

"Where are the police when you need them," I said speeding, doing 100 mph; hoping the police would pull me over so I can have them look in the trunk of my car to see who was in there, while I was still driving 100 mph; speeding, crying, and I kept looking in the rear-view mirror to see if someone was back there. As I made it home, I was disappointed that I did not see not one police car as I flew in my driveway and jumped out the car and ran to the back of the car and froze.

"What if someone is in my trunk when I opened it up," I said with a bat in my hand because, I kept one in my car on the floor. "Girl, open the trunk real slow. No! No, wait. What if they try to take the bat out of my hand when I open the trunk? Ok, plan B, call the police and have them check out the trunk. No, wait. I am about to wet on myself, I am scared and I don't see any of my neighbors out. Okay, here you go Maxine. Open the trunk real slow and keep the bat high away from the trunk so whoever is in the trunk, won't try to take the bat out of my hand," I said as I was having a lot of conversations by myself. So, I slowly opened up the trunk; nothing, there were nothing in the trunk. I was relieved as I hurried up and ran in the house, locked the door and turned on the alarm.

Fast forward to Friday: As I left work thinking about what that voice said, *"Do not go to church, do not move your car."* I went home, took a bath, put on my pajamas and slippers, wrapped my head up in a scarf and went down in the basement, sat on the sofa with a book in my hand to read and to make sure that I didn't go anywhere just like the voice said. And, because I had a dream last night that me and my youngest son was sitting in an insurance office talking to a lady and the next thing I knew, we both got up and walked out the door; then I woke up from the dream.

While I was sitting in the basement reading a book, in walks my youngest son with his friend from church. As they sat around, watched TV, in walks my middle son and said, "Dee, I need the keys to dad's truck, him and your brother just left the Detroit Pistons game and as soon as they got on the freeway, they caught a flat."

As my youngest son handed him his dad's keys to his truck, my middle son left. My cell phone rang. "Maxine, hey girl. Is my son over your house?"

"Yes, him and my son just got here about 10 minutes ago, they're here in the basement watching TV," I said.

"Maxine, they told me that they were going to McDonald's and were coming right back, I knew they probably went to your house because they were gone too long. Tell my son to come home right now," she said.

"Debbie, I don't know how he's going to get home, my middle son just came over and took the keys to his dad's truck from them. His dad caught a flat tire leaving from the Detroit Piston's game and he had to go and get him and my oldest son," I explained to her.

"That's not my problem, my car is not moving so he better get home now, can you bring him home?" she asked.

"No, my car is not moving neither," I said while thinking about what that voice said.

"Mom, please can you just let me drive him home? I promised to come right back, please mom," said my youngest son.

Now, I am mad because I remembered what the voice said to me, *"Do not go to church, do not move your car."* So, now I am thinking, the voice was only talking to me; it told <u>me</u> not to go to church and not to move my car. "Here I said, take my car, go straight there and come right back, do not make no other stops, come right back. I am not playing with you," I said as I handed him the keys to my car.

"Thanks, mom. I promised, I am coming right back," he said and left.

"Maxine, did they boys leave yet or are they still there?" She asked.

"Girl, they just left and should be there in five minutes," I said.

Ten minutes later, Debbie calls me again and said, "Maxine, the boys haven't made it here yet and I have a feeling that something bad happened."

"Debbie, I got that same feeling too," I said.

"I am on my way over your house so we can both go and look for them," she said.

"Okay, I'll be ready when you get here," I said.

My phone rings it's Debbie; again. "Maxine, I found the boys while I was on my way to your house, they got into an accident in your car. Girl, your car is messed up and they can't get it to start back up, you're going to have to call a tow truck and have it towed. It looks like they hit about five to six parked cars, they messed them up as well. I am going to leave your car here and bring your son home."

"Okay, thanks Debbie," I said.

The next day, I called off from work and had my car towed to a mechanic shop for them to give me an estimate to see how much damaged had been done to my car, then I had to get a rental car to get around in. Then me and my youngest son had to go down to the car insurance office and explain to them about the accident that he had in my car. Now, just last month, I had all three of my sons taken off of my car insurance because the insurance was too high with three teenage boys under 21 on my car insurance, I couldn't afford to pay the car insurance with them on it. I had them change their address to their dad's address. Once inside when it was our turn to stepped up to the window, we both sat down at the window and after I had explained to the lady about the accident, she was very angry with me.

"You called us last month and had us take your son's off of your insurance policy, because you said that they no longer lived with you; they lived with their dad. We took them off of your policy, so help me to understand how your son had an accident in your car, when he doesn't live with you anymore and was not supposed to be driving your car," she said.

I had to try to lie my way out of this. "I was asleep and I didn't know that he had come over and taken my car without my permission," I said.

"I think that you are lying, so I am going to pull your address. And, if their driver license is showing that they live at your address, I am going to add them back onto your policy and that's $3,000 per child and we can even get you for fraud for lying about them staying with their dad and not driving your car. Sit right here until I go and pull your address," she said.

As my son and I waited for the young lady to come back. "Your address does show only you live there and since your son took your car while you were sleeping without your permission, and because you been with us for a while and this is your first accident, I am going to cut you some slack. I was ready to throw the book at you. Because you have full coverage, bring us an estimate of the damaged done to your car so we can take care of the repairs. The next time one of your son's get caught driving your car while living with you or not, we will prosecute you to the fullest and take you to court for fraudulent," she said.

My son did almost $4,000 in damage to my car, it was in the shop for three weeks; my insurance company paid for the repairs and my son's dad got them their own cars so I know longer had to worry about them driving my car again. The six parked cars that my son had ran into, I never heard anything from anyone about that accident.

The next time I hear a voice say, *"Do not go to church, or go anywhere for that matter and do not move your car,"* trust and believe me you, she and her car AIN'T going nowhere. That was God speaking to me, He warned me twice; in my car and in my dream and I still didn't listen. Talking about the Mercy of God, that was nothing but God having mercy on me.

# EXHIBIT TWO:

# *"A FOOL AND HIS MONEY WILL SOON DEPART."*

*"If your wealth was easy to get, it will not be worth much to you."*
*Proverbs 20:21*

One day, I got tired of looking at my neighbor's backyard, he had two cars parked back there that haven't ran in years and about 30 black bags of trash behind his house and in both cars. I decided to hire someone to put up a privacy fence for me; one day while driving, I saw this guy putting up a privacy fence in this person's backyard. Every so often, I would ride past the house because I wanted to check out the progress of his work and I wanted to see the finishing result. As he was finishing up the final touch, I stop and asked him how much he charge and ask him for his business card.

Two weeks before approaching him, I heard God's voice. *"A fool and his money will soon depart."* I didn't know why God spoke that to me, even though, I was curious. So, when I asked this guy for his business card, he asked me where do I live so he can come by my house and look at where I wanted the privacy fence to be put up at and he can give me an estimate of how much it's going to cost me. Well, he came over gave me an estimate and came over the next day to get started.

After, he finished putting the privacy fence up, I hired him to fix up my basement because he wanted to fix it up for me and said that he can give me a really good deal. One month later and he's still working on my basement and I asked him what's taking him so long to finish the basement, he said that he has to wait for me to get home from work which is late; sometimes, I would come home on my lunch break and let him in the house so he can hurry up and finish my basement. He claimed that he was going to do something really nice for me for my birthday out of his own money for the basement and asked for a key to my house.

"No," I said. I would come home on my lunch break to let him in.

One day I came home early unexpected and he didn't hear me come in the door; obviously, because he had my TV on, the volume was up loud. As, I went down in the basement, he was using my washer and dryer and I saw a lot of black bags all over the basement floor. When the boys finally came home, I told them to clean up the basement and move all of those black bags from all over the basement floor.

"Mom, that's not our stuff, that's that dude stuff," they said.

I asked him what was he doing because it appeared to me that he was slowly trying to move in. "Max, my apartment caught on fire, I have been living in a motel and was wondering if I can live here until I find me somewhere else to live," he said.

"Where are you going to sleep?" I asked.

"I can sleep in the room in the basement," he said.

"I don't think so, my middle son sleeps down here in the basement, and I am not moving him out of his room; besides, I had my cousin build that bedroom just for him because he wanted to sleep in the basement, and you definitely not sleeping in the bedroom with me," I said.

"Come on, Max. Besides, you are going to be my wife," he said.

"Did God tell you that?" I asked.

Swallowing really hard, "No. But you need a man in this house," he said.

"You are right, I do need a man in this house but if God did not tell you that, then you are not the one and it's not going to happen. When I first met you, you told me that you were a minister and I have never once heard you mention God's name not one time. I asked you what church you go to and you told me two or three different names, I heard you singing while you were working on the privacy fence, I will give you credit; you can really sing. But you have been over my house working now for almost four months, it doesn't take that long to work on this small basement," I said.

"Max, if your house burned down, I would let you and the boys come live with me," he said.

"Me and my sons are just fine, God got us," I said.

"Can I at least stay here until I can find me somewhere to go? Your house is the perfect size for me," he asked.

"No!" I said.

After that he didn't come over for two weeks, then he called me and ask me to meet him at the house to let him in, so he can hurry up and finish my basement because he was working on other people's houses while he was working on my house and that he was behind on his jobs and he claimed that he was sick. After, I got home from work, he was still in the basement working and had a young lady over my house in which he claimed was his daughter. He had left and brought her over after I left to go back to work and went and got her so she can help him organize my closet in the basement, under the basement stairs, that he had closed off and built for me; she did look like she could be about 15 or 16 years of age and she did clean out and organize the closet for me.

One day, while I was at work, he called me and said that I had brought the wrong material and asked me for the receipt to take them back. When I got home, we took the materials back and exchanged them for a different material. Then he would call me at work again and said that we brought the wrong material again.

"Why don't you just let me hold onto the receipt and I will go and exchange everything while you are at work," he said.

Finally, I got fed up with him and said, "Why are you keep having me buying all the wrong materials; only to have to keep running back to the store and exchange stuff?" I asked.

He claimed that he measured the wall wrong, the material was too small. So, he had to go and get another piece of wood and get it cut bigger. Then he asked me to loan him $800 and he will buy everything while I was at work and he has to do some work at someone else's house and that client owed him money and that he will pay me back the same day because he is going to stop by his house first and collect his money so, he can pay me back when I get off of work.

When I got home, he handed me a check for $2,500 and I asked him what was this for, he claimed the client paid him in check; instead of cash. The check was made out to CASH, he had the nerve to ask me if I can cash it for him and that he will split it half with me. I played stupid! I noticed that the address on the check was right down the street from my job. So, I took the check to work and made a copy of it.

After leaving work, I went over to the address that was on the check and a couple of white men came to the door.

"Can we help you?" they asked.

"Sir, do you recognize this check?" I asked.

"Yes, that's my check.  How did you get that?"  One of the men asked.

"I have this guy working on my house and he owed me some money and he said that he did some work over at your house and you paid him in check instead of cash," I said.

Looking at each other, one of the men said, "A guy was over here doing some work but I don't know how he got my check, he did ask if he could use the bathroom and he must have snuck in my bedroom while I was outside and stole one of my checks," he said.

"Well, here is your check back," I said.

"Ma'am thank you so much for bringing us back our check and for being honest, that was very nice of you," they said.

"You are welcome," I said and left to go home; only to see the thief at my house, working.

When I got home, my neighbor next door liked how he did my privacy fence and asked him, if he could come over and give her an estimate of how much he would charge her to clean out her gutters. When he left to go next door, my house phone rang, I didn't recognize the phone number on the caller ID.

"Hello," I said.

"Ma'am, you don't know me but do you have a guy over their working on your house?" He asked.

"Yes," I said.

"Ma'am, that guy was over at my house doing some work and he stole from me; he's a thief, don't let that guy in your house. He asked to use my phone while he was here, I didn't know who he was talking to but I heard him say that he was on his way over to your house. After he left, I dialed back the phone number, I dialed *67 to warn you and that's how I was able to call you," he said.

Now I used to work at the telephone company, so I know he was telling the truth, "Thank you sir for calling me and warning me, I appreciate it," I said.

While just finishing up the phone call, my oldest son came to me and said, "Ma man, you need to get rid of that guy. I was down stairs in the basement watching TV when that guy came downstairs in the basement where I was. Ma, did you give that guy a key to the house or something? I don't know how he got in, I thought it was one of my brothers coming down the stairs. Ma, I had just got out of the shower and had my boxer's on and that guy came down in the basement looking at me like I was a piece of meat or something, asking me, did I miss him. Man Ma, I got so scared that guy was going to do something to me," he said.

"No, he does not have a key to the house that I am aware of. But you don't have to worry about him anymore, he won't be coming back over here," I said.

His truck was parked in my driveway, so I had to wait for him to come back to my house. Now, I know this guy carries a gun on him and he's at least six feet and seven inches tall and probably weighs around 350 pounds, a real big and tall guy; so, I played it real cool. I acted like I didn't know what was going on, so when he knocked on the door to tell me that he was leaving, all of a sudden, my neighbor's daughter and her boyfriend pulled up in the driveway and called him over there to the house and the next thing I knew, I heard a lot of yelling and screaming.

I stood in the door to try to hear what was going on. "I am going to call the police," I heard my neighbor's daughter say.

"Call the police, I will shoot you and everybody over here," I heard him say as he walked over to my house, reached under the seat on the driver side of his truck and got his gun and was getting ready to go back over there when all of a sudden, he immediately jumped in his truck, backed out of my driveway really fast, riding across my front yard grass. My neighbor was standing outside talking to the police and she came and asked me how well did I know the guy that was doing work on my house because she always seen him doing work on my house. I told her that I saw him doing work on someone else's house and hired him to do work on my house and I only known him a little over four months.

"My mom said that she paid him $3,000 cash to clean her gutters and I know good and well that it doesn't cost that much money to clean gutters, he took advantage of her because she is a senior citizen and he probably already peaked that her memory wasn't all that well. He claimed that he only charged her $1,500 and that she insisted to pay him up front, when he haven't done no work on her house. My mother insisted that she paid him $3,000 and when I asked him for all of the money back, he refused and said that he was going to kill all of us over here and that's when I called the police. He heard me talking to 911 and he ran from my yard in a hurry, jumped in his truck and hauled his butt out of your driveway, running over your grass," she said.

"I heard all of the screaming and yelling and I didn't know what was going on, thanks for letting me know but you definitely don't have to worry about him coming over here again," I said.

I immediately called a locksmith and had them changed the locks to my house, then I called him and said, "Your work here at my house is done, don't come back to my house anymore."

"I am coming back over there and finish what I started," he said.

"If you step one foot on my property, I will call the police on you," I said and hung up in his face. He kept calling me back, I never answered anymore of his phone calls.

The next day, I felt like something kept telling me to look inside of my garage because I haven't parked in there for a while for almost four months since he was over my house doing work, he parked his truck in my driveway; blocking my garage door. So, when I let up the garage door, I couldn't get inside my garage because he had so much stuff in there.

Now, I had wrote down the man's number from my caller ID that had called me to warn me about him, so I called him and told him that I got rid of the guy and noticed that he had a lot of stuff inside my garage and that he was welcome to come over to my house and get whatever was in there that was his. "Thanks Ma'am, that won't be necessary, I am not going to worry about it. I am just glad that you got rid of the thief, you have a blessed day and thanks for calling me and letting me know," he said as he hung up.

I worked at a bank for five years so I knew immediately that was a stolen check and this idiot tried to get me to cash it, so I can go to prison. The bank would have came after me if I had cashed that check because I would have been the one to cash a stolen check. After I told the thief not to come on my property anymore and if he did, I was going to call the police; all I had to say was police and I knew he wasn't going to come around anymore. This man was working on a lot of people's houses while he was working on my house, so that's why he wasn't coming over regularly, talking about, he was sick. And, the bad thing about that was, he was stealing from everybody whose house he was working on and storing all of his stolen goods inside of my garage. And that explains why he parked his truck in front of the garage, blocking the door, so, me or my sons couldn't get in the garage; I had the locksmith put a dead bolt on the side door of the garage as well, just in case the thief came back while I was at work.

Although, I heard God's voice two weeks earlier, before I ever knew this man, say, "*A fool and his money will soon depart.*" I did lose money dealing with this thief; however, God did warn me and once again, I did not listen to the warning. Shots fired, boom! Stupid me.

# EXHIBIT THREE:

## *"THE TONGUE OF FAITH."*

*"But without faith it is impossible to please Him: for he that cometh to God must believe that he is, and that he is a rewarder of them that diligently seek him." Hebrews 11:6 (KJV)*

One day, I noticed that whenever I prayed and asked God for anything, He always granted it to me through my husband.  I would pray and the very next day, my husband would come to me and give me what I had prayed and asked God for. I am sure, he wasn't aware that it was God who made him give it to me.  I was angry at God for blessing me through my husband, I wanted my blessings to come directly from God himself and not my husband; so, my stupid self-decided to asked God why, "God, why every time I asked you for anything, you always blessed me through my husband?"

God never answered me back, which was a good thing for me because He could have stopped my blessings all together. So, on this particular day, my oldest sister came over to my house and I was so excited to share with her how good God has been to me.

"God has been so good to me, every time I asked Him anything, He would always bless me with it," I said.

The next day, my oldest sister came back over, but this time with her daughter. I had noticed that every time I started talking, my sister would nudge her daughter; with her elbow.

"Why is it every time I start talking, you nudge your daughter?" I asked.

"I can't lie, you kept talking about how God always answered your prayers, so I went home and prayed and ask God why He always answers your prayers and not mine," she said.

"I was shock, He immediately answered me and He said your name. *"Maxine has a tongue of faith, and you only have a tongue of heart,"* she said.

"God, what do you mean by that?" She asked.

*"She believes before she asked of me; whereas, you only believe in your heart,"* she said that God had told her.

"God, why did you bless her with the house, the cars and a job and not me?" she asked.

*"You are my first born, you have my blessings,"* said God to her.

I explained to her like I explained to the youth at church. Sis, I said, "Exercising your faith in God is the same way as when your back hurts and you go to your medicine cabinet and you get a bottle of pain pills, but, before you even take the pain pills, you already have faith in it. You already know that before you take it, your back will start feeling better. Well, faith works the same way, before you go to God to ask Him of anything, you have to believe that He already answered your prayers. You have to have faith; faith is what's going to activate your prayer, and bring it to past. Without faith, it's impossible to please God. God just wants us to trust Him. Will you just have faith and trust God? All you need just like in the Bible in Matthew, Chapter 17, verse 20 says, "if you have faith the side of a mustard seed, you can say to that mountain, move and it will move." You just need enough faith about the side of a period at the end of a sentence, just that small and watch how God move on your behalf," I said.

*Jesus answered, "You were not able to make the demons go out, because your faith is too small. Believe me when I tell you, if your faith is only as big as a mustard seed you can say to this mountain, 'Move from here to there,' and it will move. You will be able to do anything." - Matthew 17:20 (ERV)*

"Okay, thanks for sharing that with me," she said.

# *"JEHOVAH JIREH, MY PROVIDER."*

*16. "Then Jesus took the five loaves of bread and two fish. He looked up into the sky and thanked God for the food. Then he broke it into pieces, which he gave to the followers to give to the people. 17. They all ate until they were full. And there was a lot of food left. Twelve baskets were filled with the pieces of food that were not eaten." - Luke 9:16 – 17 (ERV)*

One day after my two oldest sons had gone off to college and my youngest son was still living at home with me, we were having financial struggles. I didn't have a lot of my money and we were living off of McDonald's dollar menu, I decided one day that I was tired of eating McDonald's and wanted some real food; a home cooked meal to be exact. I knew my sisters were struggling as well.

I remember coming up as a child, my mother moved us from Florida to Michigan with four small daughters; all under the age of eight years old, and living with relatives at first until my mother's cousin let us live in his house; we were so excited, we had never seen snow before in our life; we couldn't wait to see the first snow fall.

My mother had no job and we had no food to eat; we didn't have the privilege of having food to eat every day, like normal people. Sometimes, for two to three days, we went without food; my mother didn't have a job, no welfare assistant and she never received child support from our dad.

A lot of times I would hate to see night time come, I would bawl up in a fetus position and just cried myself to sleep because the stomach pains were just too unbearable; I couldn't wait for morning to get here, so we could go to school and get the cold free lunches that we had finally got approved for. But there was only one problem, we were not allowed to eat our cold free lunches at school, we had to bring them home and share them with my mother and our baby sister, who was very sickly as a child; she was the reason we had to move to Michigan, she was born with a bad heart and had to have open heart surgery. The doctor said that her heart was like a sponge, it had so many holes in it and they were not expecting her to live past twelve years old.

So, we had to relocate to Michigan from Florida because Florida didn't have Open Heart Surgeons back in the 60's to operate on her heart. And, my mother couldn't afford to travel back and forth to Michigan to take care of her heart problems; so, we permanently moved to Michigan where she spent the first three years of her life in Children's Hospital of Detroit before she was allowed to come home, for the first time. She had so many blood transfusions and they had to take her heart out and physically sit it on a table next to her hospital bed; because every day, the doctors had to patch up the holes in her heart, her heart was forming so many holes. For every two holes they patched up, four holes would form, and for every four holes they patched up, eight holes would form and for every eight holes they patched up, 16 would form, etc., etc., etc., you get the picture. She faced so many heart challenges when she first entered into this world and after being in the hospital for the first three years of her life, once she came home, then she started having seizures.

Well, on this one particular day, we didn't have anything to drink or eat in our house and this elderly white couple lived directly across from us; probably in their late 70's or early 80's back then had this dairy company deliver milk, cheese, juice and eggs to their house; they had this little opening on the outside of their house where the dairy company that delivered it would put their dairies in once a week.

We hadn't eaten for at least a couple of days, and was very hungry; so, on this one particular day, they weren't at home and my mother told me and my oldest sister to run across the grass and steal it; we were so scared and didn't want to do it but our mother made us do it. So, my oldest sister and I ran across the grass as soon as the Dairy truck delivered the goods and pulled off, we took their milk, eggs and cheese and anything else that was in the outdoor shoot. My mother had us do this for weeks, as soon as the Dairy truck pulled off, we would run and hurried up and grab their goods.

Well, on this one particular day, right after the Dairy truck pulled off, we got caught. As soon as my sister and I grabbed the goods, had them in our hands, we turned to run back across the grass only to see the elderly couple, sitting in their car, just staring at us, watching us take their goods. They never said not one word to us, they eventually moved and we never saw them again.

Being hungry and growing up poor was a generational curse that I didn't want my sons to experience, but my ex-husband left me no choice and I was too embarrassed to tell my sons about the financial struggles that I was facing; after divorcing their dad and not to mention that Chrysler wanting to garnish all of my pay check for a leased vehicle that he had set on fire, that I had just leased from them and was facing foreclosure as well. I had very little money and food but managed to scrape whatever little food in the house was available to eat. I knew my sisters didn't have much and was probably hungry as well; so, I decided to cook and invited my family over to eat.

My youngest son said, "Mom, we barely have enough food for you and me, how are you going to feed everybody that you invited over? Your three sisters and your niece and me and you, that's six people. Mom, look how small the pots are, there's hardly any food in any of the pots, what are you going to do, give everybody a teaspoon of everything from each pot?" he said.

"Wow! I didn't realize how little food it was. Oh, well, I already invited them over now; so, I am just going to bless the food and pray that anybody that walks through the door, that God multiplies the food, so everybody can eat," I said.

Everybody that I invited came over and I told them to fix their own food and get as much as they wanted. Let me tell you, not only did God showed up, but He showed out; everybody ate, some ate seconds and took a plate of food home to eat for later. Five days later, my youngest son and I were still eating leftovers from that day; all of a sudden, we both stopped eating and looked at one another.

"Mom, wait a minute, is this the same food that you cooked five days ago where there was hardly any food in the smallest pots that we had and where your sisters, your niece including me and you ate and everybody ate until they got full and took plates home and five days later, you and I are still eating left overs?" asked my youngest son.

"Yes," I said.

All of a sudden, we both stopped eating; at the same time. We both looked up to heaven, at the same time; and we both turned our heads and looked at one another at the same time.

"That was nobody but God," we both said at the same time, as we looked down at our plate full of food; at the same time.

# EXHIBIT FIVE:

## *"THAT'S NOT CHICKEN."*

*Leviticus 11:1-47*

Now, my youngest son had left home and I am now an empty nester. I still go down stairs in the basement and watch TV, the basement was like our family room where we spent 90 percent of our time. Whenever the boys had company, everyone knew the basement was the hang out spot. Even though, my sons were grown and gone, that still was my hang out spot. The Detroit Pistons were my favorite team, before Joe Dumar, split the team up. I had prepared myself for this game. I can't remember who they were going to play that day but, I intentionally starved myself all day so I can eat and watch the basketball game; my mouth was watering for some Chinese food, I already knew exactly what I wanted.

The game started at 7:00 p.m. and at 6:00 p.m. I ordered me a General Spicy Chicken, I think it was a #3 combo with chicken fried rice and an extra sweet and sour sauce from my favorite local Chinese Restaurant, Wong's in Lincoln Park, Michigan; they have the best Chinese food ever. I haven't had them in a while so this was going to be a treat myself day, as my stomach was starting to growl; making all kind of noises because I was getting so hungry from not eating nothing all day; waiting for the game to come on. I went to go and pick up my order and made it back home just in time because the basketball game was getting ready to start.

As I sat down on the sofa and turned the TV on, my stomach was smelling the food and was really cutting up, growling so loud. I couldn't open the container fast enough to hurry up and stuff my mouth. Just as I was about to put the food in my mouth, a voice came from out of nowhere; now I know I am not crazy, but I could have sworn that it was just me and the house; home alone. *"That's not chicken,"* said the voice.

I froze on the sofa, too scared to move when I heard the voice speaking to me. I slowly looked down at my food; staring at it real hard to see if it were chicken or not, and trying to make sure that my food didn't start moving. The voice came from the left side of me as if someone was standing right there next to me, now my stomach was really starting to make weird hungry noises.

I thought to myself, 'Man, something watched me all day, let me starve myself and waited until I went and got my food, knowing that I was hungry, and as soon as I was just about to put the food in my mouth, it said, 'that's not chicken.' As I sat on the sofa and stared down at my food, my stomach started growling, louder and louder.

"I don't care right now, I am hungry," I said.

The voice said it again but this time louder, more firm and angrier, *"That's not chicken!"*

I knew then that I had made whoever or whatever that was, mad. I slowly and gently closed the food box. I slowly and gently picked up the remote control, while slowly cutting my eyes in the direction from which the voice came from; not seeing nothing or anybody in that direction; I was trying hard not to even breathe hard in fear of whoever or whatever it was, to not make it any angrier.

I slowly and gently walked over to the TV and turned it off and laid the remote control on top of the TV and walked very slow and soft and threw my food in the trash can where we kept it by the end of the basement stairs and hauled my butt up the basement stairs; I didn't know at that time that I could run that fast, not looking back. I was praying the whole time that whatever it was, that it wasn't running up the stairs besides me and was not at the top of the stairs, waiting on me. I never went back down in the basement to watch TV again, I only went gently down the stairs looking around trying to watch my back at the same time, to wash my clothes.

I bought a brand-new TV, I put it in my bedroom, but I ended up having the military get the TV and the bedroom set from which my middle son had from him sleeping in the basement and shipped it to my oldest son who is in the military, I gave it to them because they had just brought a four-bedroom home; moving from a one-bedroom apartment. In the summer time, I slept down in the basement in his bedroom because it was cool in the basement, and I moved back upstairs in the winter.

When I told my youngest son, what happened about the Chinese food, he said, "Mom, I think it got angry at you because it was looking out for you, and you said that you didn't care because you were hungry and you were going to eat it anyway."

My son was right, I am sure whatever it was, was looking out for me. I didn't eat Chinese food again for years after that incident; yep, I'm good!

"I am never going to eat Chinese food ever again," said my youngest son.

# EXHIBIT SIX:

## *"GOD LOOKS OUT FOR FOOLS AND CHILDREN."*
### *– Meshell Ndegeocello*

Coming up as a child, I would always hear my mother say, "God looks out for fools and children." I would often times hear her say this whenever my sisters and I did something wrong. This day my youngest son was going to a gun and knife show at a Trade Center in Novi, Michigan. He asked me if I wanted to go with him.

"Yes," I said.

Once there, I figured, I better get me a stun gun and a small pistol to carry in my purse because I lived alone and the neighborhood was just starting to get bad; they were doing home invasions, breaking into people homes in broad daylight, while people were in their home; so, I needed some kind of protection. As I filled out the application for them to do a background check on me, I was so happy I got approved; I couldn't wait to get my gun registered and take shooting lessons.

As the man that sold me the gun was explaining the gun rules to me, I couldn't wait to get home to learn how to use my pistol. My youngest son came over to show me how to load and unload the magazine and told me that there is always one bullet in the chamber, and don't forget that whenever I am unloading or cleaning my pistol, to take it out and keep the safety lock on whenever the grandchildren are over. I told my son what the man that sold me the gun had said.

"Mom, don't listen to that man, he told you wrong. Don't take your gun down to the police station to register it, only take the piece of paper that he gave you showing you purchased the gun," said my youngest son.

Before leaving for work the next morning, I unloaded my pistol and put the safety lock on and left the key to the lock at home.

"My son doesn't know what he's talking about, telling me to not bring my pistol down to the police station. I am going to listen to the man that sold me my pistol, he would know more than my son would," I said to myself.

So, I decided to take my Pistol after work to get it registered, I put the pistol in my glove compartment and went to work; I left work a little early than usual that day before going down to the police station, I wanted to get there before they closed; so, I can register my pistol.

As I pulled into the parking lot, my knees were starting to bother me; but you couldn't tell me nothing. I had just got myself my first pistol, and I just turned fifty; I was feeling very powerful. You couldn't tell this sister that she wasn't bad; bad knees, in all. Before getting out of the car, I took the pistol out of the glove compartment, put it in my purse.

As I got out of the car trying to figure out which door to go in, the security guard flagged me down. "Ma'am, you can go through this door, I see that you have bad knees like me and I didn't want you to have to walk all the way around to the front."

"Thank you so much, sir," I said.

"What are you here for?" He asked.

"I am here to register my gun," I said.

"Once you go in these doors, go straight to the left and go in the double doors and the registration office is right there," he said.

*"GOD LOOKS OUT FOR FOOLS AND CHILDREN," I heard my mama say.*

That's weird, I said, "Why did I just heard my mama's voice."

As I was just about to open the door, a really nice police officer was walking out and he held the door open for me.

"Thanks," I said.

As I went to the left and entered through the double doors, a lady officer said to me, "Sign in and someone will be right with you."

As I finished signing in, I took my pistol out of my purse to lay it down on the counter top. The next thing I knew, I was surrounded by at least twelve police officers, pointing their guns at me. "Hold it right there, put your hands up and step away from your Pistol and your purse," said one of the police officers.

With my hands up in the air, I starting crying and said, "I just wanted to register my gun."

"We don't care. Who do you think you are walking in here with a loaded gun? Keep your hands up where we can see them. You just stand right there and don't move," one of the police officers said, as all twelve cops were still pointing their guns at me.

"I just wanted to register my gun," I said, still crying.

One of the police officers asked me, "How did you get in the building with a loaded gun?"

"The security guard let me in through the back door," I said.

"So, let us get this straight, you came in through the Employee's Only entrance, by-passed all of the metal detectors, came into the office and pulled out a loaded gun. How did you get here?" the police officer asked.

"I drove myself," I said.

"Where was your gun?" He asked.

"In my glove compartment, I just wanted to register my gun" I said, crying even harder.

"Ma'am, you can stop with the crying, we don't care. You think just because you have a cute face in all, that we are going to cut you some slack; just three months ago, someone off of the streets, just like you, walked in here, by-passed all of the metal detectors, just like you and open fired in this building and killed two of our police officers. So, we don't care nothing about your tears or your innocence little cute face; right now. You are facing a felony. You drove here with a loaded gun in your glove compartment, within reaching distance and walked in here illegally through the 'Employee's Only' entrance, took the pistol out of your purse, so, we automatically assumed that you were going to open fire," the police officer said.

"The man at the Trade Center told me to bring my gun down to the police station to register it, I just wanted to register my gun," I said, still crying.

"What is the man's name that told you to bring your gun down inside of a police station to register it? You don't have to bring your gun here; all you need is to show proof that you purchased it. I want to know the name, address and phone number of the person that sold you the gun, he should have known better to tell you that; he is going to be in a lot of trouble for telling you to bring your gun down to a police station," the police officer said to me; yelling.

The next thing I knew, they escorted me out into the hallway. While I was standing there crying, I noticed they had cleared the building out; nobody was in the hallway but me and the janitor. The janitor leaned over to me and handed me some paper towels to dry my face and then he whispered to me and said, "Ma'am, what did you do?"

As I was explaining to him what happened, he said to me, "You see the white guy standing over there staring at you?"

As I looked up from crying and saw the white guy just standing there staring at me, "Yes," I said.

"That's the police chief, they called in the top dog on you. I know that look, he's examining you. Whenever he stands afar off, nine time out of ten, he's not going to charge you. Today is your lucky day, I think he's going to let you go; I don't think he is going to put you in jail," said the janitor whispering to me.

After the police chief walked away, a police officer walked up to me and said, "Here's the deal, the police chief has decided to not charge you with a felony, he has decided to not throw you in jail, even though, you by-passed all the metal detectors and walked in here with a loaded gun. He said that he doesn't think that you had any intention of doing any harm because you did have the safety lock on and he said that he thinks that you forgot to remove the bullet from the chamber; so, for those reasons, he has decided to not charge you. You are free to go home but we have to escort you out of the building, you are not allowed to touch your gun; we are going to put it in the trunk of your car for you," he said as a lady officer came and handed me my purse.

"I don't want that stupid gun anymore, I just want to go home," I said and started crying again.

"Ma'am, you can't be afraid of your gun. Come back here in two weeks to pick up your permit for your gun; you can drive to a gun range and practice shooting your gun without having your permit; you have to get familiar with your gun. If you don't want it, today is my birthday and I will be happy to buy it off of you," said the female officer.

They put my gun in a box, taped it up so I couldn't get to it and put it in the trunk of my car and told me to go straight home. I cried all the way home and once I got inside my house, I immediately called my youngest son on the phone and told him what happened.

"Mom, man. I told you not to take your gun down to the police station, I told you to just take the piece of paper that you purchased the gun with; it has all the information on it," he said.

"I thought you didn't know what you were talking about; so, I listened to the man that sold me the gun," I said.

"Yes, and see where that got you. Mom, they could have charged you with a felony and once they charged you with a felony, that could have messed you up for the rest of your life; a felony doesn't come off of your record. You would have lost your job and no one will probably never hire you, ever again. You said that you heard your mama's voice saying, 'God looks out for fools and children,' that was God talking to you in your mother's voice and once again mom, you didn't listen," he said.

Y'all, let me tell you guys how stupid I felt; okay. I walked in the police station, feeling like a powerful 50-year-old but I walked out of there feeling like a five-year-old; crying like a baby. More shots fired, again! Boom! #StupidMe

# EXHIBIT SEVEN:

# *"WRESTLING WITH A SPIRIT."*

### *Genesis 32:22-24 (ERV)*

*22. "During the night, Jacob got up and began moving his two wives, his two maids, and his eleven sons across the Jabbok River at the crossing."*

*23. "After he sent his family across the river, he sent across everything he had."*

### *The Fight with God*

*24. "Jacob was left alone, and a man came and wrestled with him. The man fought with him until the sun came up."*

I had just awakened when I heard my oldest sister's voice, *"Maxine,"* she said.

I'm thinking to myself as I immediately got out of bed looking through the house, 'Mary is in my house? How did she get in my house? I didn't know that she has a key to my house.' After searching throughout the entire house, I didn't see anyone so I went and laid back down in the bed and the voice called my name again, *"Maxine."*

"Whatever!" I said turned my back and threw the cover over my face. The next thing I knew, something leaped on me. I was wrestling with this thing, trying to get it off of me but it was super strong and when I tried to see what it was, it held my face down into the mattress so I couldn't see it. So, as I manage to get one of my hands free, I tried to grab it by the hand but my hand went right through it.

"You are a Spirit, I am not afraid of you," I said as I continued to wrestle with this thing for at least ten minutes trying to get loose and to see its face, but this Spirit was super strong and refused to let me up, let alone, to see it. Ten minutes of wrestling with this thing, felt like eternity. The next thing I knew, it was gone just like that. Once I was able to get up, I sat on my bed in shock trying to figure out what just happened and what was that. I immediately got dressed, grabbed my purse and my car keys and left.

I went over to my mother's house and told her what had just happened and she said, "You are not going back over to that house, you are staying over here." I stayed four days over at my mother's house and had to go back home because I needed some clothes to wear, I didn't grab anything after the incident happened; only my purse, my car keys and left with only the clothes on my back and hauled butt out of that house. After wrestling with whatever it was, imitating my oldest sister's voice, it never said anything else to me while wrestling with me; holding my face down into the mattress so I couldn't see it. I knew it was a Spirit because every time I tried to grab its hands to try to get it off of me, my hand just went right through it. It could touch me, but I couldn't physically touch it.

My mother and my sister went over to the house with me, we had hammers, bats and knives, as I unlock the door, we all went into the house at the same time; we went in every room of the house making sure that nothing or no one was in the house. I was tired of sleeping on my mother's sofa so, I stayed home and I never heard my oldest sister's voice, calling me again.

When I told my youngest son about what happened, he said, "Mom, I don't think whatever it was, wanted to hurt you because if it wanted to hurt you, it could have. I think it only got angry with you because you said, 'Whatever!' turned your back and threw the cover over your face.

# EXHIBIT EIGHT:

# *"GOD HAD ALREADY WORKED IT OUT, WHILE I WAS TRYING TO FIGURE IT OUT."*

*"Trust in the LORD with all thine heart; and lean not unto thine own understanding." Proverbs 3:5 (KJV)*

On this particular day, we had gotten about at least eight feet of snow, it was dark outside. I was coming home from work on this winter day and I saw all the men outside shoveling their snow, my yard was the only one that wasn't shoveled and I didn't know any of them well enough to ask them to help shovel my snow and they never volunteered to help. So, as I was coming down the street and saw how high the snow was, I wanted to cry because I wasn't sure if I was going to be able to get into my driveway.

As I attempted to pull into my driveway, my car got stuck between the street and the beginning of the driveway; so, I put the car in reverse to try to get out; it wouldn't go, then I put it back in drive to try to make it go and it wouldn't go. I did this repeatedly about 30 minutes with the car rocking back and forth, making loud noises and nobody came over to help me. I know they could hear my car stuck in the snow and they just kept on shoveling their snow and when they had finished, they all went inside their houses while, I was still trying to get up in my driveway.

The back end of the car was hanging halfway out in the street, and I couldn't get the car to move up; so, no one coming up or down the street would hit my car. I finally stopped trying to pull in the driveway because I noticed that by me gunning the gas pedal down to the floor, I was only wasting a lot of gas. I was hurt and angry that no one came over to help me, the men after finished shoveling their snow, could have at least, came over and tried to push my car out of the street for me; that would have made me feel better. When I looked up, I was the only one left outside; so, I grabbed my purse, bags and cane and fought my way through the snow and made it to my side door and went in the house.

As I sat by my big front window, eating my food and looking out the window to see if anyone was going to come outside to shovel my snow, it was getting late; 11:00 p.m. and no one never came back out. I was trying to figure out in my mind how I was going to be able to go to work, that was a lot of snow; and, I didn't know anyone to call to help me. I said to myself, 'I am going to have to get up real early like 3:00 a.m. to try to shovel my way out; so, that I can at least try to make it to work on time. I have a forty-five-minute commute, and, that's without any snow; so, I know it's going to take me at least two hours and that's taking my time, so I wouldn't have to rush. I will get to work earlier than usual, but that will be okay; unfortunately, the problem is that there are bats in the building. If I am the only one in the building and I see a bat, Lord, help me; I don't know what I'll do. Maybe, I will just sit in my car and wait until the appropriate time and then go inside when others arrive.'

I couldn't sleep wondering how I was going to make it to work, I tossed and turned all night; maybe, I can just call off sick, I am thinking. That would be the easiest way out; but first let me get up early and try to shovel my way out. As I hurried to bed so I can get up early, I woke up at three a.m. put on the proper clothing, to try to stay warm; while, I am getting ready to go outside to shovel eight feet or more of snow.

As I walked out of my door, I was startled. As, I stood in my long driveway by the side door, I was trying to process what happened. Someone had shoveled my entire driveway, all the way back to my garage, my sidewalk; even, my front porch. They shoveled the snow in the street for me as well and cleaned off my entire car. Hallelujah! Thank you Jesus, God is good. So, I went back inside the house to get me a couple of more hours of sleep. I woke up, took my bath, got dressed and got in my car and drove off to work.

I cried again but this time, it was tears of joy, I was so happy. I didn't get any sleep because, I was trying to figure out how I was going to shovel my way out and make it to work on time. "While I was trying to figure it out, God had already worked it out," I said to myself.

And, He didn't just stop there, all winter or whenever we had snow, a bad snow, a snow storm or even a blizzard, I would wake up only to find my driveway, sidewalk, porch and even my car already cleaned off. God is good all of the time and all of the time God is good. All winter long, I had been trying to find the mystery person who was heaven sent to help me. I would wake up early and stayed up late just to try to find out who it was; as soon as I fell asleep, I woke up only to have my snow shoveled.

One Saturday morning, I heard someone outside of my window, shoveling my snow. This was the day that I was going to figure out this mystery person, who God had sent to help me. It was my new neighbor next door, they had just moved over there; and, I was mad that this man and his family had moved next door to me; because his sister had stayed there a couple of years before she moved out, and I would see him over there visiting her at times. She kept a lot of female company over there; even though, they kept to themselves, sometimes, they got a little loud.

I just know they had traffic coming and going all day and all night long; so, I automatically associated him with her and was very angry that he had moved next door; which, was wrong on my part.

Little did I know, him and his family was the best thing that ever happened to me; the loud noise and traffic stopped, and I never had to worry about my grass getting cut; every time he cut his grass, he would cut mine. Every winter, he shoveled my snow and cleaned off my car for me so when I woke up to go to work, all I had to do was get in my car and drive. He did this all the while I lived there and whenever I tried to offer him money, he would smile and say, "Girl, gone with that. I am not charging you anything; keep your money. I can't have my yard looking nice and your yard looking crazy, that would make my yard look bad," he said, smiling as he was walking away and went inside of his house.

So, whenever I saw his wife outside, I would call her over and give her the money to give to their son and daughter; so, they can start them a little savings. She was just like her husband; she didn't want to take the money neither but I insisted that she give it to the kids. I found out that he had brought the house and let his sister and her three daughters live there, but her female friends kept up a lot of loud noise; so, she moved back into an apartment and him and his family moved into the house that he brought from the previous neighbor that lived there; they both worked together at Ford Motor Company and he was having financial problems; so, my neighbor bought the house from him to help him out.

You can't tell me that God is not good, I was praying for the old neighbors to move because they kept filling my garbage can up with their garbage; so, on garbage day, I didn't have nowhere to put my garbage. And, they were tearing up my grass by allowing their grandchildren to play in my yard; and not theirs. I had prayed to God for them to be gone, and God answered my prayers. All this time, *God had already worked it out; while, I was trying to figure it out*. Amen.

# "TAKE NO THOUGHT OF WHAT TO SAY."

*25. "Therefore I say unto you, take no thought for your life, what ye shall eat, or what ye shall drink; nor yet for your body, what ye shall put on. Is not the life more than meat, and the body than raiment?"*

*34. "Take therefore no thought for the morrow: for the morrow shall take thought for the things of itself. Sufficient unto the day is the evil thereof." Matthew 6:25 & 34*

One night while sleeping, God showed me in a dream, me on the job and my boss came to my desk, and sent me on a different floor to work called, 'Dispatch.' Now, I didn't know what the dream meant; until after I went to work. After getting myself situated upon arriving to work, my supervisor walked up to my desk and told me that she was sending me on the eleventh floor in the Dispatch Department to work, they needed help doing payroll and she chose me to go and help them out; just the way God had showed me in the dream.

Once, I cleared out all of my things from the desk, my supervisor took me on the 11th floor where I will begin my new job assignment. I would be reporting to two area managers, working directly under them. They immediately called a floor meeting and asked everyone to meet outside of the door by their office; there were probably about sixty-eight employees on that floor, whereas, my previous job, it was only six of us clerks; so, this was a bigger floor and more people.

"Everyone, this is our new Payroll Clerk, her name is Maxine. She will be working strictly under us; she will not be answering to no managers or anyone. Managers are not allowed to ask her to do anything, but the managers will be answering to her; we are putting her in-charge of this entire floor. So, if you guys have a question for us area managers, you can go to Maxine and she can come and relay the problems, questions or any concerns to us. This will cut down on some of the traffic coming in and out of our office; so, we will be able to get some of our work done," said one of the area managers.

"Who is this new person again?" asked one of the employees.

"Her name is Maxine," said the other area manager.

"What's her title?" asked another person.

"That's none of your concern right now, we haven't figured out a title for her yet; we haven't figured out exactly what she will be doing just yet, she just got here. Now, everyone let's all welcome Maxine, and get back to work," said the area manager.

Well, my first day here and I did not get a friendly welcome, no one came to welcome me in my new department; they only stared at me. The area managers called me into their office and told me to close the door behind me. As I closed the door and sat down, they pulled out this report.

"We have this report that we look at daily but neither one of us can figure it out; so, we are going to need you to figure it out, and send us a daily report. Send it to us and we will forward it to all of the managers so they can cover their employees on this report. And, you will be doing payroll for sixty-eight employees; that's every employee on this floor; except the managers. Everybody else that we've hired, could never figure out this report, so we are counting on you to not let us down," they said and handed me the report and told me to go on line and take a tutorial course to learn how to do payroll.

Well, needless to say, that was all of my training. Even though, we are not supposed to take our work home, I took the report home and asked my sons to help me figure out the report. They looked at it and said, "Mom, this report is easy." They explained it to me and helped me set up the report according by managers and their direct reports, that we listed under them; and, we color coded the report by Managers and their employees.

Wow! The next day, I took the report to work, I never told my two new bosses that I took the report home and had my sons help me figured it out and the truth be told, I was truly embarrassed to even show them the report because it was not good news at all. This report showed everything; what time a person signed in to start working, what time they signed out for lunch, what time they signed back in coming back from lunch, and the time they signed out for the day to go home; it was a wonder if anybody on this floor still had a job.

"Well, we sort of figured that this is what was happening on this floor but we had no way of proving it; you are a genius, nobody could never figure out this report. Make sure you send us the report every morning; to us only, not the managers. We don't want them to know that the report is coming from you, there are going to be a lot of changes around here; maybe, some people are going to lose their jobs," they said.

After my meeting with them, they called a floor meeting with everyone; including, the managers. "Everyone, starting today, there will be new rules that everyone; including the managers will have to follow. There will be no more coming into work late, you must be at your desk and signed in no later than five minutes early to start working and signed out to go home, no more than five minutes early to go home. Anything earlier than that, your paycheck will be docked fifteen minutes; so, we will take fifteen minutes of your pay and your pay check will be short. You must sign out on time for breaks and lunches at your assigned time. If you are at your desk and forget to sign in or out, your pay check will be dock fifteen minutes for every five minutes late signing in and docked thirty minutes for every fifteen minutes late signing in or out, and, so on. If you sign in early more than five minutes, because we know some people get here early, and signs in thirty minutes early which means that we have to pay you overtime and since we are not approving any overtime at all, we suggest you don't sign in no more than five minutes early and don't sign out more than five minutes early or you will be written up; after being written up the first time, it's a verbal warning. The second time, a written warning, and the third time, there will be a three-day suspension, with no pay and/or dismissal from the company. And, if you are not putting in the correct time on your timesheet, you will be falsifying your work hours and you will be dismissed from the company," said the area manager.

No one was happy about that meeting. So, after the meeting, I think my bosses set me up on purpose; they sent out the original report that I send to them, to the managers; either by accident, or on purpose. Either way, it caused a lot of problems for me on my job. The managers went and told their employees about the report that I sent to the area managers; and, that's how they knew what everybody on the floor were doing, from the time they signed in to come to work and from the time they signed out for the day; they had alarmed their employees about me sending out that report.

The managers came up to me and said, "That's not right what you are doing, sending out that report. You are going to get all of our asses fired."

"You're going to get your own asses fired, I am not losing my job for no one; especially, by falsifying information and not putting it on your payroll; that's stealing money from the company. I am only doing what I was told to do; so, go and talk to your boss; if you have a problem," I said.

My bosses called in the office and said, "Maxine, we are truly sorry. We accidentally sent out the original report with your name on it to all of the managers; if anybody says anything to you, please come in our office right away and we will handle it from there. We didn't realize that we did that until one of the managers came into our office and asked why the report had your name on it. We are truly sorry for throwing you under the bus, we messed up."

Well, I was disappointed that they did that and I didn't know what to say. The next thing I knew, a Union Representative approached me and said, "What you are doing is not right, we are demanding that you stop doing that report immediately or else you will be reprimanded and no union person in this entire company will ever represent you."

"I am only doing what I was told to do," I said.

"We understand that, but you are doing the work of a manager, and you are not a manager, nor can we pay you for doing the work of a manger," said the Union Rep.

After that, my bosses asked me to focus on doing payroll only and had me to show them how to read the report and they will send out the report from here on out. I had never done payroll before in my life; so, I asked one of the managers to help me and I overheard one of the other managers say while trying to whisper in the other managers ear, "Don't help her; since she's so smart, let her figure it out herself."

No one on the floor would help me, they were really nasty to me and did everything in their power to try to get me fired. When it was time for me to go home, they would wait until I got close to the elevator and closed the door in my face; I could hear them all laughing as the elevator door closed. While at work, passing out pay checks or distributing company mail to everyone, I noticed every time I walked pass this one girl's desk, she would say, "Man, I feel like fighting!"

# "PUTTING YOUR MOUTH ON A CHILD OF GOD."

*23. "Elisha went from that city to Bethel, He was walking up the hill to the city, and some boys were coming down out of the city. They began making fun of him. They said, "Go away, you bald-headed man! Go away, you bald-headed man!"*

*24. "Elisha looked back and saw them. He asked the LORD to cause bad things to happen to them. Then two bears came out of the forest and attacked the boys. There were 42 boys ripped apart by the bears."*
*2 Kings 2:23-24*

So, I was not sure if she was talking to me or not. I tested her to see if she was talking to me, I would purposely dress up; I wore my skirt set and my high heels and purposely walked past her desk; again. She would say the same thing; again, this time louder to make sure that I heard her, "Man, I feel like fighting."

Sometimes, she would put her chair in the middle of the isle to block me from walking past her desk, I pretended that her and her chair was a ghost and just politely moved her and her chair and kept it moving. Now, this girl could have been Beyonce's little sister, she had a bad body and shape on her, but her attitude was jacked up. She would get up in the middle of the floor and started twerking and the managers would start laughing; I guess they thought she was cute and funny, they never did or said anything to her.

So, the next day, I dressed up again. I heard the managers say, "Grandma sure be dressing up, she comes to work every day, dressing sharp; her outfit, shoes and her purse all match. We are going to have to step up our game."

I was sending a message to Beyonce's little wannabe sister, that anytime she wanted to fight, I was ready; I was going to fight her dressed up in all. So, when I purposely walked past her desk again, she didn't block the isle with her chair this time but rather sat right by her desk so I can see her staring at me.

So, she said it again, "Man, I feel like fighting."

This time, I stopped right in front of her desk, looking her in her eyes and said, "Any time, you feel froggish; leap b**ch!"

After work that day, I was so in distress and upset, and was tired of the mess that was happening on my job; I was truly fed up. As soon as I stepped foot inside my house, I laid on the living room floor and cried out loud to God, "Lord, you sent me to Dispatch. You showed me in a dream that I was going to work in that office. Lord, you are going to have to help me figure out how to do payroll, nobody will help me and everybody is rude and nasty to me. Lord, Father God, I need you to help me; I am tired of the people messing with me and every time, I walk past this girl's desk, she always wanting to fight me; Lord, please help me."

The next day, the Lord showed me how to do Payroll, it came so easy to me and one of the other Manager that had whispered in the other Manager's ear and told the other Manager not to help me; but, rather let me figure it out myself; since, I was so smart, walked up to me and said, "I thought you said that you didn't know how to do Payroll, can you help me with one of my employee's time sheet? I can't figure it out."

"Pray and ask God to help you; or better yet, figure it out yourself; since, you are so smart," I said as I walked away, wanting her to know that I heard what she said while she was trying to whisper in the other Manager's ear.

She ran and told all of the other Managers what I said, the looks that I got from the Managers; if only, looks could kill; they would have killed me.

One day, while sitting at my desk doing Payroll, and not paying any attention to what was going on, on the floor; out of nowhere, I heard God's voice.

*"Take no thought of what to say," he said.*

To make sure that I heard Him correct, I said, "What?"

*"Take no thought of what to say," he said, again.*

The next thing I knew, one of the nice managers, that actually liked me, came and tapped me on the shoulder and said, "Maxine, they want to see you in the big conference room."

As I followed him in the conference room, I saw the entire floor in there; including all of the employees, all of the managers and both of the area managers, that I work for, all sitting in there. As, I walked in there looking around at everyone, some of the managers and employees would frown their faces up at me and turn their heads to keep from looking at me.

"Come in Maxine and have a seat. I guess you are wondering why everyone is in the conference room," said one of the area managers.

I never noticed that I was the only one on the floor; until, the manager came and got me. Then I reminded myself of what God said, *"Take no thought of what to say."* So, I said within myself, 'Maxine, don't try to figure out what this meeting is about, just sit here and listen.'

"As you are unaware of, every day, the managers and their employees come into our office all day, complaining about you. We can't get any work done because they are in our office saying, "Maxine did this or Maxine did that." So, we decided that since they were complaining about you from the start of the day until it's time to go home, it's only fair to call a meeting with you included; since, they wanted to have a meeting without you. So, the floor is open, anybody that has a problem with Maxine, here's your chance to speak up, and tell her what your complaints are against her," said one of the Area Managers.

As I sat there waiting to hear what they had to say about me, you can hear a pen drop; it was just that silent. "Let me rephrase the question. Everyone that has a problem with Maxine, raise your hand," said the area manager.

Not one person raised their hand. Both of the area managers looked at one another and said, "We don't believe this, everyone in this conference room have been coming into our office; every day, all day long; keeping us from doing our work and complained about you and now that we called a meeting, not one person has anything to say. From here on out, not one of you better come into our office and tell us anything that Maxine is doing or has done; as a matter of fact, we better not hear y'all mention her name or we will write every one of you up. So, here's your last chance to speak up, anyone who doesn't have a problem with Maxine is free to leave the meeting right now," said the area manager.

Everyone in the conference room, all sixty-eight employees; including all the Managers, got up quickly and ran out of the conference room.

"Wait a minute, Gladys; you, and Steve get back here right now, you guys were the main ones in our office complaining about Maxine every day," said one of the area managers. The managers never came back but just kept walking out of the conference room.

"Didn't we just tell Glady's and Steve to get back in here and they ignored us and kept walking out of the Conference room," said one of the Area Managers.

"Yes, we did," said the other Area Manager.

"So, now, we are going to write them up for insubordination."

A couple of the managers got fired, Gladys retired and Steve was let go from the company; someone filed a sexual harassment law suit against him. One of the Area Managers, that I worked for, retired from the company; while the other Area Manager, got transferred to a different location. All sixty-eight employees; including myself, were sent to work at a different location. At the new location where they sent us all to work, I was still doing the same thing- payroll, but this time for almost 300 employees. Even though we worked on different floors, I still did their payroll and they made everyone that had five years or less, managers. I had twenty years and they over looked everyone with high seniority.

One day, while, walking into the building, one of the co-workers from the previous job stopped me and said, "Maxine, girl. I have been looking all over for you in the company. Do you remember that girl that couldn't stand you; every time you walked past her desk, she wanted to fight you?"

"Yes, I remember," I said.

"Girl, I don't know if you heard or not, but she's sick; she has some kind of flesh-eating disease, she can't walk. She's in an electric motorized wheelchair and she had just had a baby not too long ago, under two-years-old," my co-worker said.

"Wow! I didn't know that; I feel bad for her, I am sorry to hear that," I said.

One month later, I ran into my former co-worker again. "Maxine, remember when I was telling you about the girl who didn't like you and she always wanting to fight you every time you walked pass her desk, and she came down with some kind of flesh-eating disease and couldn't walk and was in an electric motorized wheelchair."

"I remember," I said.

"Girl, she died."

# "GOD SENT A PROPHET TO WARN ME."

*"TOUCH NOT MY ANOINTED, AND DO MY PROPHETS NO HARM."*
*PSALMS 105:15*

I took some time off from work because I was having two different surgeries; having my gall bladder taken out, and having fibroids removed; both at the same time. While I was home recovering from both surgeries, I had a dream whereas, God showed me at work sitting at my desk, but I didn't recognize anyone on the job, and then, I woke up.

Upon waking up, my phone rung and it was a Union Rep from my job calling me at my home to inform me that once I come back from my disability leave, I will no longer report to Southfield, Michigan; I will be reporting to Pontiac, Michigan. Ten months later, after I returned back to work from my disability leave and returned to my new job in Pontiac, the people already did not like me because I had over 25 years of seniority on my job and they had less than 15 years.

These people were worse than the people I worked with in Downtown, Detroit and in Southfield. Here I go again, every time, God show me in a dream of Him sending me to work at another job, within the company; the people got worse. Once again, the harassment started, the lying started all over again, not to mention, they tried to get me fired; all because I was number three on the top of the seniority list.

"When are you going to retire?" a co-worker asked.

"When everyone on this floor is gone," I said.

I became frustrated and fed up with the bullying and harassment; so, after leaving work, and, as soon as I entered into the door, I laid on my living room floor and cried out to God; again. "Father God, I am so tired of the people on my job. You sent me to this place with nasty and rude people, why is it Father God, that every time you send me somewhere or anywhere in the company to work, the people get worse? How much longer are you going to make me do this? I want to retire. I am tired of going through this, I am an adult and is being bullied and harassed everyday on my job," I said, as I cried out to God.

Well, to relieve some stress and to take my mind off of the job, I decided to surprise my family and make personalize calendars for my entire family. After I finished making the calendars, I decided to go to Staples on top of the hill in Allen Park, Michigan to have them put in wire binders so they can look more professional. It was a really bad day that day, but I was super excited of having the personalize calendars finish so I can give them to my family.

There were lots of snow on the ground and it was very icy; as well. As I pulled up in Staples's parking lot and parked the car, I noticed another car pulled up at the same time as I did and parked directly in front of me. As I proceeded to get out of the car, being extra careful to not fall and I was looking down at the ground; as well, trying to make sure that I didn't walk on any ice; all of a sudden, I heard a loud voice say, "You be careful mama, don't you fall."

I jumped so hard because I truly did not know who the young man was talking to as he got out of his car; he startled me. So, as I was looking around trying to see who this young man was talking too.

"I am talking to you mama, don't you fall," he said to me.

As I hurried inside the store, the young man and the young lady walked up to me. "I am so sorry Mama; I didn't mean to scare you. This is my wife; she has MS and we both are youth pastors. We live in Southfield, Michigan but God told us to come to this Staples here in Allen Park, he wanted me too talk to you. He said that, you are a preacher and that you will be preaching for Him," he said.

"Yes, He showed me in a dream, up in the pulpit at a Church, preparing myself to preach. As, I was pacing back and forth across the pulpit, I was trying to hear a word from God. I said, 'Ok God, you sent me here to preach to the women. God, I need to hear a word from you. I need to know what it is that you want me to preach to the women about. God, tell me what to say," I said, as I was looking out in the sanctuary, at the men and women who was staring at me; waiting for me to start preaching. I know, I said, "God wants me to preach to the women, on how to love their husbands," and then I woke up," I said to him.

"God told me to tell you that your family doesn't like you, and they are not your family. God said that He only brought your mom and dad together for one reason; and, that was to bring you forth into the world; but they are not your family. God also wants me to tell you that the people on your job are messing with you, and lying on you. God said, if they don't stop messing with you, if they don't stop lying on you, He will come down from Heaven Himself and splatter them every which-a-way," said the young Prophet.

*"People will insult you and hurt you. They will lie and say all kinds of evil things about you because you follow me. But when they do that, know that great blessings belong to you." – Matthew 5:11 (ERV)*

After that young Prophet, prophesied to me, the very next day at work, it appeared my co-workers knew something bad was going to happen to them if they didn't leave me alone, so, they eased up on me. I was scared for them, a little bit and at the same time, I wanted to see them get their reward; I wanted to see God come down from heaven and splatter them every-which-a-way. The truth of the matter is, I just wanted them to leave me alone; and, stop lying on me. God sent a prophet to warn me of what He was going to do to them, if they didn't take their mouths off of me and stop lying on me. Thank you, Jesus; because, I just couldn't take it anymore.

# TAME YOUR TONGUE

*But no human being can tame the tongue. It is a restless evil, full of deadly poison. James 3:8 (ESV)*

# "GOD KEPT HIS WORD."

*"So shall my word be that goeth forth out of my mouth: it shall not return unto me void, but it shall accomplish that which I please, and it shall prosper in the thing whereto I sent it." Isaiah 55:11 (KJV)*

My mother and I talked every day on my lunch break at work; on this one particular day, my mother called me and asked me, "Maxine, you always say that God talks to you, how do you know it's God that is talking to you?" she asked me.

A month later, my mom called me at work very excited. "Maxine, I finally heard from God. I heard God's voice," she said.

*"Cora, I'm coming for you,"* she said, that *He said.*

"Maxine," she said again, even more excited. "God said, He is coming for me; He is coming for me."

My heart sunk; she obviously didn't know what He meant, but I did.  Every day, I remembered what she said, and every day, I tried to watch for a sign from God; scared and nervous. We had just developed a mother and daughter relationship, and we were in a good place.  I never held the past against my mother, I never brought up the past; and, we never talked about it. I was just happy to have my mother talking with me and us spending quality time together. I didn't care how she treated me in the past; after all, that was the past and I left the past, in the past.

I always said to myself, 'You only get one mother and after she is gone, you don't get another one.'  So, I am going to just love her and kill her with kindness. I never disrespected her and I only talked back once to her, in my whole life; only to defend myself, when she called me out of my name.  Even, while I was grown, I never disrespected her, nor talked back to her; I feared God.

I remembered God's Fifth Commandment; *"Honor thy father and thy mother: that thy days may be long upon the land which the LORD thy God giveth thee."* I did not want my days to be cut short from talking back, being disrespectful or being disobedient to my mother.

We talked every day and I told her that I was going to retire soon; May 15, 2017, the exact date. And, that I am going to take her anywhere in the world; wherever, she wanted to go.  She was so excited and said, "I want to go and visit my sisters." I was retiring just for my mother, I wanted to see her happy; I had never seen my mother happy, only struggling to care for and provide for my sisters and I.  And, because God had showed me in a dream, in a church, in the pulpit, getting ready to preach; I was going to take my mother everywhere with me, to see her sisters and travel the world with me; while, I was preaching for God.

Unfortunately, God came for her just like He promised; He kept His word. She passed away on my youngest son, De'Andre's, birthday; and, three months before I retired.  She did, however, made things right with me before she passed away; she apologized to me for how she treated me. She told me that she loved me. And, she said, "Maxine, I thank God so much for you. You have been nothing but a blessing to the entire family and you helped everyone in the entire family out and we treated you wrong, please forgive us." I never held a grudge against anyone; not my mother or my sisters; so, no apology needed, it's all good. It's all love, God got us.

# "A TRIBUTE TO MY MAMA:"

Mama, I remember the day you called me on the phone; Summer of 2016; and said, "Maxine, I don't know if I was dreaming or not but God spoke to me and said, "Cora, I'm coming for you." Mama, on Friday, February 10, 2017 a little after 9:30 p.m. God came for you, just like He said; He kept His word. He took you, Mama, so you His precious daughter wouldn't have to suffer no more. He took you, Mama, before the worse got worst.

Mama, God gave you to us (your daughters; Mary, Maxine, Valerie and Carolyn); your grandchildren (Takeisha, Wardell, Jr. and his wife Jessica, Isiah, Sr. and his wife Chaquita, De'Andre and his wife Darlena, and Klyn; everyone's favorite and heart, (may your soul R.I.H with God) and your Great-Grand Children (Zaya, Isiah, Jr., A'Niyah, Ian, Jayla, Julian, Zoey, Jade, Nolan and Wardell, 3rd) for a reason and a season, but it was never meant to be for a lifetime; because, you belong to Him; you are His child. He took you, Mama, so you no longer have to worry no more.

No more sickness, and no more pain.
No more crying, and no more dying.
Mama, you made it! He's giving you eternal, everlasting life.
And, for that reason Heavenly Father, Lord Jehovah, I say, "Thank you." Thank you for loaning us your precious daughter, Cora; also known as, Mama, Grandma, and Gigi.
Mama, God kept His word; He came for you just like He said.
Loving you and missing you dearly, Mama!

Always in our hearts, gone too soon. Always loved and never forgotten.

Crying from a broken heart. 

May your soul Rest in Heaven with God, Mama.
Cora J. Henderson
July 28, 1940 – February 10, 2017

And, may your soul Rest in Heaven with God, Son, Nephew & Cousin.
Klyn Javon Bullock
September 27, 2002 – August 21, 2019

# "I SHOOK HEAVEN."

*12. "Our fight is not against people on earth. We are fighting against the rulers and authorities and the powers of this world's darkness. We are fighting against the spiritual powers of evil in the heavenly places.*

*13. That is why you need to get God's full armor. Then on the day of evil, you will be able to stand strong. And when you have finished the whole fight, you will be standing." - Ephesians 6:11-13 (ERV)*

After retiring from my job, I was home more and strange things started happening. I woke up one day and froze dead in my tracks. I tried hard not to breathe but fake like I was still asleep. I didn't know what was going on; but there were two spirits in my bedroom, I felt their presence so strong; I was terrified. I said to myself, "Don't move Maxine, fake like you are asleep."

As, I laid there terrified, I had fallen back to sleep; only to wake up again, with those two spirits still in my bedroom; I knew exactly where they were in my bedroom. I am thinking to myself; this is weird. I usually can tell what type of spirits that I am dealing with but I am sensing one is a known spirit and the other is an unknown spirit. As I laid in my bed trying not to panic, I felled asleep again, when I woke up this time, they were gone; thank you, Jesus. I did not get a good feeling about those spirits.

One day, as my usual routine, I put my car inside the garage for the weekend. After coming in the house from putting my car inside the garage, I was in the bathroom getting ready for bed and before I could finish up in the bathroom, something startled me; I jumped so hard. Now, I didn't see anything but I could feel an evil presence standing right in back of me, I mean this thing and I were literally standing not even a foot apart; even though, I couldn't see it, its evil presence was so strong. I didn't know whether to do number one or number two on myself because its presence was not a good feeling. 'Maxine, if you never needed God before, you need him now. You are going to have to use every scripture that you know, to fight against this thing,' I am thinking to myself.

As I was standing there thinking about Ephesians 6:11-12 (KJV) in my mind, verse 11 says, "Put on the whole armor of God, that ye may be able to stand against the wiles of the devil. For we wrestle not against flesh and blood, but against the rulers of the darkness of this world, against spiritual wickedness in high places." So, as I turned around to face this thing head on, I said to myself, 'Maxine, you can't show no fear; otherwise, this thing will rip you apart. You're going to have to be bold and stand up to this thing; you're going to have to use every scripture that you know to use, to fight this thing, you're in a spiritual warfare.' As I got up the nerve to take on this evil spirit, face to face, toe to toe because I was the only one in the house, I lived by myself; all of my sons were grown, married and gone. I knew that I was in trouble at this point and had to call on God. The next thing I knew, I started screaming at this evil spirit from the very top of my lungs.

"I AM NOT AFRAID OF YOU! YOU ARE MESSING WITH THE RIGHT PERSON! DO YOU KNOW WHO MY FATHER IS? DO YOU? BECAUSE IF YOU DID, YOU WOULDN'T COME HERE! YOU WOULD NOT HAVE BOTHERED ME! I AM A CHILD OF THE MOST-HIGH GOD! NO WEAPON FORMED AGAINST ME SHALL PROSPER! YOU CAN'T TOUCH ME, satan (I spelled it with a small 's' because, I have no respect for the devil)!

YOU HAVE TO GET PERMISSION FROM GOD TO TOUCH ME, YOU ASKED GOD FOR PERMISSION TO TOUCH ME AND HE SAID, 'ACCESS DENIED.' SO, YOU-CAN'T-TOUCH-ME! GOD HAS NOT GIVEN ME THE SPIRIT OF FEAR BUT OF POWER, OF LOVE AND A SOUND MIND! I HAVE POWER OVER YOU satan! SO, GET AWAY FROM ME IN THE NAME OF JESUS! IN JESUS NAME, satan, I AM NOT AFRAID OF YOU; YOU DON'T BELONG HERE! IF YOU KNOW WHO MY FATHER IS, THEN YOU WOULD NOT HAVE COME HERE! MY FATHER IS JEHOVAH GOD! AT THE NAME OF JESUS, DEMONS, TREMBLE AND FLEE! SO, GET AWAY FROM ME satan!

YOU HAVE NO RIGHT BEING HERE! HEAVENLY FATHER (I said while still screaming from the top of my lungs; so loud, I am sure the neighbors probably heard me and was wondering who I was arguing with), I NEED YOU TO COME DOWN

FROM HEAVEN, RIGHT NOW LORD. THIS BATTLE IS NOT MINE; THIS BATTLE BELONGS TO YOU. THIS BATTLE IS TOO BIG FOR ME, PLEASE COME DOWN FROM HEAVEN LORD AND FIGHT THIS BATTLE FOR ME!" I said, still screaming so hard and so loud that I was mentally and physically exhausted; almost, losing my voice and breathing hard like I was in a physically fight with this thing. In my mind, I saw what you would consider like a Lochness Monster, or something so demonic and evil, super tall, long face, with super sharp teeth, standing toe to toe in front of me; I really can't describe what was going on spiritually, but I knew I couldn't allow fear to take over.

As I stood there for a moment, trying to get a hold of myself, I realized that this thing was still standing in the door of the bathroom and I had to walk pass it to go inside my bedroom. So, I had to put on the whole armor of God; again. I had to make sure that I didn't show no fear. I was so angry at this thing, I checked out mentally and just lost it. I almost forgot that I was standing face to face by an evil spirit but, I didn't care at that moment.

I boldly walked past whatever it was and went in my bedroom, sat on my bed and was breathing harder than ever, from screaming at this thing. I picked up the remote control and turned on the TV, thinking that I was going to calm down, relax and chill and that this thing was going to flee. But, no, this thing wasn't going anywhere; all of a sudden, it started thundering and lighting real hard; I had never heard it thunder and lightning this bad before in my life. Before I knew it, all the power in the house went out, I had no lights at all.

While sitting on my bed in the dark, I picked up my phone and called a friend of mine who deals with these types of spirits and when he answered, I didn't say anything, I just pointed the phone in the direction of the evil spirit.

"Maxine! Oh, my God! Get out of the house now. You are in serious trouble, I will explain to you later, just get out of the house now."

"Okay," I said as I hung up the phone and called my youngest son to come and get me. I am not sure when he came to get me and I had put my car inside the garage and I had no way of getting to it; because, I had no power; then I realized that my son couldn't come inside because I had put the dead bolt lock on the side door and only I had a key to that lock.

So, as, I was reaching in the dark trying to find my purse, my cell phone fell out of my hand  and onto the floor.  I almost wet on myself and wanted to cry because I knew then that I was really in trouble. I had to bend over in the dark to try to find my cell phone. I was thinking this thing can bust me in the back of my head and kill me.

As I was reaching down, I kept my head up high to try to see where this thing was at; I finally found my phone, grabbed my purse and was trying to figure out how I was going to walk past this thing in the dark; hoping and praying it wouldn't attack me. The thundering and lightning were getting worse than ever; I don't know which were scarier; the thundering and lighting or this thing.  I used the light on the phone to find my way out of the house and praying that I didn't see its face.

As, I finally made my way to the side door, I unlocked the door and ran out the door as fast as I could and got in my son's car; once inside the car, I told him to pull off and drive as fast as he could out the driveway.

"Mom, what's going on?" He asked.

"I'll tell you later, just drive," I said.

As soon as he pulled out of the driveway, all of the sudden, the thundering and lightning stopped. As we were going down the street, I noticed that my house and three more houses next to me on the left of me on the block were the only ones that had no power; my good neighbor, that is always helping me, had power; every light in his house was on. My entire block had power; all the other houses on the next blocks over had power; it was just my house, and three other houses; that was without power.

My friend called me and said, "I am just checking to make sure that you made it out alright. Maxine, I don't know if you could hear that thing or not but it was so demonic that I dropped the phone; that scared me. Whew, the sound of that thing, I am surprised you made it out alive."

"I didn't hear anything and thank God, I didn't hear it; my heart probably would have stopped beating," I said.

When I explained everything to him that happened, he said, "You shook heaven. You called on God and God came down immediately through the thundering and lightning and was whipping that thing's behind; that's why it didn't touch you. God caused the power to go out; so, you couldn't see his face. God came down from Heaven because you called on him to fight that battle for you. God was detaining that thing, that's why it couldn't touch you as you walked past it, in the dark; that's the only reason why you were able to get out of the house alive," he said.

After telling my youngest son what had happened, for once, he was speechless; he had no comments.

# "SPEAK IT INTO EXISTENCE."

*Speak over your life daily*

*"Death and life are in the power of the tongue."*
*– Proverbs 18:21 Amplified Bible*

*Learn to love yourself and always speak blessings over your life, your family and your loved ones. Speak this daily over your life, I AM….*

A Child of God, Amazing, Anointed, Appreciative, Awesome, Beautiful inside and out, Blessed, Caring, Confident, Dedicated, Discerning, Exciting, Excellent, Faithful, Forgiving, Fruitful, Full of Life, Genuine, Gifted, God's Masterpiece, Grateful, Happy, Healed from the crown of my head to the very soul of my feet, Healthy, Highly Favored, Holy, I Love Jesus, Intelligence, Joyful, Kind, Living in the Overflow, Loving, Merciful, Passionate, Peaceful, Positive, Powerful, Redeemed, Smart, Spirit Filled with the Holy Ghost, Strong, Successful, Thankful, Trustworthy, Unique, Unstoppable, Valuable, Wealthy, Wise, Whole, Zealous